# REVOLUTIONARY MOVEMENTS IN MANIPUR

# REVOLUTIONARY MOVEMENTS IN MANIPUR

N. JOYKUMAR SINGH

AKANSHA PUBLISHING HOUSE
NEW DELHI

**AKANSHA PUBLISHING HOUSE**
R 37-B, Vani Vihar, Uttam Nagar
New Delhi-110059
Email: ektabooks@yahoo.com

*Showroom*
4649/21B, Ansari Road
Darya Ganj
New Delhi - 110 002
Ph. : 23269193 / 9811582579

**Revolutionary Movements in Manipur**



*First Edition 2005*
ISBN 81-87-606-92-4



[ The responsibility for the facts stated, conclusions reached etc. is entirely that of the Author. The publisher is not responsible for them, whatsoever. ]

PRINTED IN INDIA

Published by M.P. Misra for Akansha Publishing House, New Delhi and Printed at Tarun Offset Press, Delhi.

*Dedicated*

*to My beloved father*

Late Shri N. Mani Singh

*A strict disciplinarian and guiding force*

*In the journey of my life*

# Foreword

It was a great pleasure for me to have gone through the book "Revolutionary Movements in Manipur" written by Professor N. Joykumar Singh, a well-known historian and an academician of commitment. This book is a study of the revolutionary political movements both at the theoretical and empirical levels. The earlier work of the author, namely, "Social Movements in Manipur: 1917-1950" deals with the anti-British and anti-colonial people's movements. The present work is an important study to understand the post-merger political movements in the state, which had two trends. The first was the peaceful agitations launched by the political parties, based on "Gandhiji's Satyagraha" to establish democratic representative form of democracy and statehood for Manipur within the Indian Union. The second one was the armed struggle for the liberation of Manipur from the so-called "Indian colonial rule" and establishment of a sovereign state outside the Indian Union. The present work of Professor Joykumar is concerned with the second category of the political movements which are described popularly as insurgency and also known in Manipur as "Naharolgi Ehou" (Movement or revolt of the youth). The movement is definitely not a youth movement in the conventional sense. It is a deep-rooted assertion of the ethnic nationalism with a clean act of revolutionary agenda. Professor Joykumar rightly described these movements as a phenomenon of "Revolutionary Movements".

This study is a well-researched and well-documented work for which the author should be commended. The scholarship and historical acumen of Professor Joykumar are unfolded in the pages of his book. The author deals with five aspects of the theme: a theoretical exposition on revolutions, the genesis of the revolutionary movements in Manipur, the nature and character of the movement, the leadership pattern and the impact of the movements. Starting with the classical definition of the revolution as "change or transformation" the author deals with a comparative theories of revolution, both Marxian and non-Marxian. If we follow the classification of the revolutionary categories one is inclined to think the insurgencies in Manipur as the guerilla-based armed revolutions based on the classification of Paul Wilkinson. The occurrence of armed revolutionary struggle was due to denial, by the imperialist or the pro-imperialist government, of the peaceful means for the masses of the people to gain national aims including armed intervention to reverse popular trend towards independence. This type of revolutionary movement uses "violence against violence" (P. 18-19). The guerilla warfare is a form of revolutionary struggle in Manipur.

The author has given an impartial and objective account of six well-known revolutionary parties, namely, The Meitei State Committee (MSC), United National Liberation Front (UNLF), Revolutionary Government of Manipur (RGM), Peoples Liberation Army (PLA) Eastern Region, Peoples Revolutionary Party of Kangleipak (PREPAK), and Kangleipak Communist Party (KCP). The writer analyses the character of the parties on the basis of the ideological perspectives. The Meitei State Committee was a legacy of the Communist movement launched by Hijam Irabot Singh; naturally the members of MSC were admirers of Irabot Singh but their ideology was a mixture of nationalism and leftist slogans. The KCP is the inheritor of the tradition of MSC. The United National Liberation Front is based on the Manipuri nationalism and common cultural heritage of the Meiteis and hill tribes. The exploit of the RGM, which was an offshoot of the UNLF, shows its similarity of the ideology plank of the original Front. They use the name "Manipur" which is not used by other parties, which used the term Kangleipak (PREPAK and KCP). PLA is purely based on Marxism. PREPAK is based on Meitei ethnic nationalism. The author gives fairly authentic presentation of the parties, their aims, objectives and their activities, failures or achievements. The UNLF appears to be the mother of the revolutionary groups. RGM broke away from the UNLF, so also the PLA. Both PREPAK and KCP are independent of UNLF.

The analysis of the role of leaders and the pattern of leadership is a major contribution of the book. The author examines the role of Arambam Somorendro, the leader of the UNLF, O. Sudhirkumar of the RGM, N. Bisheshwor of the PLA, R.K. Tullachandra of PREPAK and W. Tomba of the Meitei State Committee. The author writes of Arambam Somorendro as a man of complex personality, a thinker, writer, a sports lover, a great playwright and a good social worker, a champion of Manipuri nationalism and a great revolutionary "ideologue". He comments on O Sudhirkumar in the following words.

"Sudhir possessed a rare quality of leadership, a wonderful commanding personality, a man of wide reading and a revolutionary nationalist". N. Bisheshwor was the founder of the Lasha-trained PLA, "a revolutionary activist and leader". According to the author N. Bisheshwor Singh fits into cloak of "a charismatic leader". While PREPAK was based on collective leadership, but during his lifetime, "R.K. Tullachandra Singh stood out as the main architect of the PREPAK". Ibohal Singh of the KCP was a product of the Meitei State Committee who possessed a unique leadership".

The revolutionary movements are still on-going current movements. They have produced tremendous impact on the polity, society, governance in the state and the psychology of the people. The Government of India was compelled by the movements to change their attitude towards the people of Manipur and the state of Manipur.

Professor Joykumar Singh has consulted the original sources of informations, in the possession of the government and the revolutionary parties. The rich information is supplemented by the extensive personal interviews with the leaders themselves. It is a fairly impartial and objective study of a very critical and sensitive theme.

I am sure this book will definitely have a wide readership in the general public, policy framers, academicians and students who are interested in the study of insurgency movements everywhere.

**Prof. GANGMUMEI KAMEI**

# Preface

The *Revolutionary Movements in Manipur* is a story of political activities of some armed revolutionary organisations launched from the pre-merger period with an objective of establishing a separate political identity of Manipur state. In one sense it is not a new phenomenon in the experience of the people of Manipur. The people of Manipur had a very good experience of the activities of various types of movements right from the British colonial rule. The outbreaks of tribal movements, peasant movements, women's movements, students' movements, religious revitalization movements, etc. were the important features in the ongoing process of the history of the state. From these evidences it can be suggested that Manipur is a hot pot of various type of social movements. The author has already done some work on the nature and character of social movements in Manipur and their impacts.

As a matter of fact everybody knows those activities of the revolutionary movements in this state even to the people of outside Manipur. I am also afraid that my work will be a repetition of the existing knowledge of the people. Actually the main objective of this work is to make a humble attempt to study the nature and character of some specific revolutionary organisations, which I always consider as pioneers in such movements. My work is also confined only to a specific period of time, which I consider as significant in the history of the revolutionary movements in Manipur. As a whole, I am trying to give maximum emphasis on the theoretical concept of revolutionary movement and an attempt is also made to analyze every aspect of the movement within the conceptual and typological framework of the theory of revolution. While analyzing the different aspect of the movement I am also trying to give a historical picture of the genesis and growth of separatist tendencies among the people of the state particularly the younger generation group. I am also fully convinced that the outbreak of these revolutionary movements has produced a lot of positive impacts in every aspect of the state including the development side also. Therefore I have devoted a separate chapter on the impact of the movement where

I have tried to highlight the outcome of the activities of the movement and its response. While analyzing the different aspects of the process of the movement I always try to make a balance observation from historical perspective and also within the framework of the concept of social movement. Another objective of this small work is to highlight some historical facts of the whole activities of the movements including their ideology so that the younger generation would be able to analyze them more critically and in a more detailed way in future. If it is so, then we would be able to give a concrete and comprehensive picture of the whole movement. I never consider this small work as a comprehensive study on the activities of the revolutionary movements in Manipur. It is just a small step towards a gigantic task of academic world.

In the process of the preparation of this small work I took help from many personalities and social activists. But due to certain limitations it is not possible to mention all their names here one by one. However, I am fully aware of the fact that without their help it will not be possible for me to make a successful completion of this monograph. Therefore I would like to express my sincere gratitude to those personalities for their kind cooperation and help.

I am also greatly indebted to Prof. Roy Burman for taking a great pain in reading the manuscript in the midst of his hectic schedule in Manipur. His suggestions and observations gave a new spirit in the process of writing.

I also thank Prof. Gangmumei Kamei, a renowned historian of the region for giving a valuable guidance in every stage of my work. Actually, his is the moving force behind this work. His inspiration has given a new spirit to my moral strength. At the same time I am also really grateful to him for writing the 'foreword' of this book.

I would like to express my sincere thanks to some of my near and dear friends and well-wishers for their encouragement and moral help. Prof. P. Nabachandra Singh, my childhood friend and professional colleague, Prof. Lal Dena, Prof. G.P. Singh, and others are some of the important established personalities who have given moral encouragement to me.

In the process of the completion of the work I also took help from many of my young friends. Shri Konjengbam Meghachandra Singh, Shri Sanasam Amal Singh, Dr. N. Debendra Singh, Shri Aheibam Koireng

Singh, Shri Bhabananda Singh, Ch. Hemchandra (Khaba), Shri H. Sudhir Singh, Salam Jiten Luwang are the key persons who have rendered a lot of physical and logistic help to me. I am really grateful to them for their valuable help.

I would also like to express my sincere gratitude to Miss Shimray, the stenographer of History Department, Mr. S. Shantibala Devi, technical assistant of the Centre for Manipur Studies, for taking a great pain in typing. Without their help I would not be able to complete my work. I also thank my office peon I. Bijen Singh for his valuable physical help to me. I am also grateful to H. Shamo Singh and Dr. R.K. Somorjit Singh for taking special care of giving a new shape in cover designing process.

However, the final shape of the work is possible when it has come out in the printed form without which the completion of this research work cannot be treated as final. Therefore, the acceptance of M/s Akansha Publishing House, New Delhi, to take the responsibility of publishing and distribution of the book is a great contribution to the success of my work. So, I would like to thank the proprietor and manager Mr. M.P. Misra of this publishing house for their generous and timely help.

Lastly, I also thank all my personal friends of various circles of social life and my wife and my children for their moral and physical contribution in the process of the completion of my work.

**N. JOYKUMAR SINGH**

# Contents

# CHAPTER ONE

# INTRODUCTION

## (A) WHAT IS REVOLUTION?

The word 'revolution' is used with different connotations according to the nature of its application. The term is derived from the Latin words 're' and 'volvere', which mean 'to turn'. So, when it refers to an action on other parts of celestial bodies and their movements from one place to another it denotes the returning or moving of an object to its place of origin.[1] But when it applies to the society and history it again carries a different connotation i.e., the degeneration of an established order and the emergence of a new one. In social science, the theory of revolution means social progress which replaces the old regime morally, institutionally and technologically to a more productive for the advancement to a superior stage in social evolution.[2] From the standpoint of the concept of the modern political movement a 'revolution' means the liberation of a nation from the domination of others. And it is an attempt to wrest the political power and social ascendancy from the ruling stratum. It is therefore suggested that revolution means a radical change by using violent method. Everett D. Martin interprets the concept of revolution as a political change involving the abolition of the traditional state authority or the encroachment on its prerogative.[3] Charles A. Ellword also suggested that the term 'revolution' should be used in a strictly political sense. He observes that revolution is a change in the power structure.[4] However, some writers are of the opinion that revolutionary changes are nothing but an integral part of long revolution. According to them the concept of revolution may be treated as one particular ingredient of social development. Hannah Arendt writes, "revolution is a form of change within the social system, not mere change, but change nonetheless".[6] On the basis of this conceptual framework revolution is a form of social change undertaken in response to specific conditions of the social system.

Apart from its relation with social system the term 'revolution' has acquired a variety of meanings: Scientific, technological, communal, financial, agrarian, educational and even sexual revolutions as well as revolution in fashion, which are distinguished as independent phenomena on the ground of their influences on society. From this point of view some western writers think that the term 'revolution' is one of the misused words and there are varieties of meaning, which make it as adaptable to personal purposes as in chameleon's skin.[7] According to Mark N. Hegopian, the word 'revolution' is a popular, even glamorous word nowadays. Thus many people overworked it until it loses all definite meaning.[8] A.S. Cohan, a British researcher, observed that the term 'revolution' has got a considerable variation in its definition. "That it may be concluded that the authors are not talking about the same phenomenon."[9] Thus the term 'revolution' and its conceptual definition embraces all the different issues in the society. The concept of technological and scientific revolution and cultural revolution, etc. are also other aspects which can be looked into and discussed from the conceptual definition of the term revolution. In this respect Mark N. Hegopian wrote, "revolution sometimes comes to embrace such phenomena on the 'Reformation' and the 'Industrial Revolution', which in fact lies outside the ground covered by the term. Even such developments in America's political life on President Roosevelt's New Deal have been given the status of revolution, e.g. the revolution of the New Deal, the Keynesian revolution etc.[10]

Such type of observations and interpretations of the western writers was regarded by the Marxian writers as 'discordance and confusion.' They said that it was a manifestation of inconsistency and absence of methodological clarity.[11] They called them (western writers) bourgeois researchers and their approach and mode of view point was termed as 'formalist stand'. The Marxian writers are of the view that the bourgeois researchers turned a blind eye to the distinction between phenomena which have vital, fundamental impact on the destinies of mankind, and those processes underway in various restricted areas of man's activity. Therefore, on the basis of this point of ignorance they are equating the basic concept of revolution with so many phenomena. They further argued that their understanding of substantial changes in either individual or even several aspects of the life of the society are far from equivalent to revolution as understood by Marx Engels and Lenin. According to Karl Marx revolutions are the 'locomotives of history,' for they blaze the road for human society, leading it from one stage of historical development i.e. the transition to the new; new socio-political and economic relations and institutions, new ideas, new ethics etc.[12] Marx thinks that a revolution is carried out by the people but the material pre-requisites for a new social system and the objective conditions for a revolution through which these prerequisites are into being in new institutions and relations are created by the objective course of social development, primarily by the development of the productive forces; at a certain stage the latters come into conflict with the existing production relations. Marx was of the view that the revolutions, which the bourgeois researchers used to call coup d'etate, do not affect the economic, political and ethical foundations of the existing social system. Revolution have some common features, but they also differ from one another in "social nature, motive forces, aims and tasks and finally, in the pattern of their emergence and development.[13]

Lenin said, "Revolution is a change which breaks the old order to its new foundation."[14] It means that it is a drastic change of an existing social system. He was of the view that to achieve the goal the revolution must tackle a wide range of concrete task, such as destruction of the old and creation of a new, consolidation of new social relations. He further said that a successful construction of socialist state could be possible only when the involvement of the working people was there. This was a difficult task. But this task cannot be fulfilled by the same force and same ways and means that were employed to solve the problems of the bourgeois revolution. To Lenin the socialist revolution differs from the bourgeois revolution not only in its aims and task and in the mechanisms involved in its emergence and evolution, but also in its motive forces, strategies or tactics. To culminate in the construction of a new society the socialist revolution embraces a prolonged, complicated and contradictory historical period. Such type of revolution, according to Lenin, would be a whole epoch of sharp class strength and many social upheavals. It is a well-known fact that destruction and transformation of the old society are the corollaries of the revolution. The socialist revolution destroys the old society much more radically than the bourgeois revolution. Therefore during the period of revolution all the social groups faced many problems and difficulties. Lenin wrote, "Everybody knows that revolutionary movements are always and inevitably accompanied by temporary chaos, destruction and disorder... Of course, the socialist revolution cannot be immediately presented to the people to a clean, neat and impeccable form".[15]

In the midst of this debate between Marxian and non-Marxian writers on the issue of the interpretation of the term 'revolution', some writers also advanced different views on the term revolution. By giving justification to the earlier observation, Hannah Arendt said that a revolution always viewed at an overthrow of the social order and replacement it by a new order. On the basis of this belief the writer took revolution as a true restoration. Some suggested that the word 'revolution' should be applied only to revolution whose aim is freedom. Mousier, a French scholar is of the view that revolution aims at erasing the real illness of the society and is always violent, because the existing authorities shall naturally resist these changes. According to Lock, if the sovereign failed to carry out the terms of the social contract and protected the natural rights of the individual, the latter was free to revolt against his authority. Therefore he strongly asserted that revolution is an instrument to protect the right of the people. Herold Laski, a modern political thinker is of the view that revolution is an attempt by the use of force against the government legally in power to compel a change in what are held to be those using such force, the actual purpose of the state. According to M.N. Roy, revolution was subversive of the status quo and reorganization of society on the basis of freedom and equality. On this point of argument he again said that revolution is an international social necessity.

Although many writers and political thinkers advanced different observations and interpretations on the term 'revolution' it can be suggested that revolution always aims at a fundamental change in the existing established order. It also aims to bring a much higher progressive plan by substituting the old system, and so it helps in eliminating the deep rooted evils in the social system and transform it into a new society. George Sawyer Peter defines revolution as 'reconstitution of the state.'[16] He further said that this type of revolution fraught with profound consequences for a given society or number of societies. The outcome of the revolution is such that the new condition of the state has nothing in common with its original structure. From this fact it can be observed that revolution is an illegal and, as a rule, violent-change of the existing form of government. In the process of the revolutionary activities the masses or ordinary citizens are affected. So revolution is the repeated sweeping change in many orders of the nature of the society by seeking a major alteration in the prevailing distribution of wealth and status of power. It is a complete overthrow of the established order and forcible substitution by a new order. Therefore on the basis of this understanding Wolfenstian defined the term 'revolution' as a form of politics characterized by the extensive use of violent or other illegal means in competition for control of government power and authority."[17]

The characters of the revolutionary movements are not at all identical. But despite the difference of patterns of revolution, there are still certain common features of the causes of the outbreak of the revolution. One important feature, which is acceptable to all, is that revolution occurred mainly due to the inefficiency of governing class and economic crisis. However, Walter Laquer is of the view that even when there is a revolutionary situation the result may not come out in the form of revolution. Sometimes it may lead to anarchy or to a non-revolutionary dictatorship if the revolutionary players are not capable of swift and decisive action.[18] According to Marxism, revolution arises in conformity with the objective laws governing the social development. They believe that economic causes e.g. a low standard of living is the genesis of the revolution. Further, they are of the view that social political and economic issues are the primary factors of the revolution. Lenin also gave an elaborate definition of the features of revolutionary situations. He cited the suffering and poverty of the oppressed class, a crisis in the policy of the ruling class, a considerable increase in the objectivity of the masses drawn into independent historical action.[19] He further said that this general law is subject to change depending on the concrete situation.

Marxian writers said that for a successful revolution there must be two revolutionary situations – highly developed productive forces and a proletariat adequately prepared for it. But this theory also was not at all correct. In this regard some writers pointed out that France in the 18th century was poor in her developmental aspect and lacked serious political organization of the proletariats, and there was no corresponding preparation, no prolonged training of the working class. It is explained that "The revolutionary situation is the process, always objective usually lengthy, and frequently contradictory, of the growth and maturing of its features.[20] Lenin also shared this view. He said, "revolutions are never born ready made; they do not spring out of Jupiter's head; they do not kindle at once."[21] From this observation it can be deduced that the stage of the slow accumulation of strength by the oppressed classes against the stable rule of the oppressors is the basic starting point of the gradual maturing conditions for a revolutionary situation. Lenin also admitted that objective changes are not the only factor for a revolutionary situation. It is to be accompanied by subjective changes. This is the highest stage of the maturing of the revolutionary situation. He further said that subjective change is an inherent feature of this situation. It contains subjective factor. Therefore Lenin called this stage as 'directly revolutionary crisis' 'directly revolutionary struggle' 'a nation wide crisis' etc.[22] Whatever the case may be the Marxian writers strongly asserted that the conflict between the productive forces and production relation is the only factor for the outbreak of revolution. The development of productive forces exerts a revolutionizing influence on all aspects of the life of the society. The conflict and clashes between the new productive forces and old production relations was acting as medium for progressive or old ideas. One group is fighting to preserve the social and political system formed on the basis of old ideas and the other groups is campaigning to abolish it and establish a more progressive social and political system on the new concept that Marxists termed as new relation of production.

By adopting the pluralistic approach of analysis the non-Marxian writers advocated that 'not a single universal method nor a single theory of revolution can be worked out'. They called the Marxist Leninist doctrine of revolution as purely 'obsolete' in the present era. They do not accept the application of the same yardstick to revolutions of entirely different types. Mark Hegopian wrote, "Modern social science teaches that highly complex events such as revolution are caused by many factors and not by a single factor."[23] He was of the view that the theory of revolution of the Marxist is of the monocausal theories, which explain the origin of revolution by the impact of economics and the existence of conspiratorial elites. He further argues that their approach is to give a rough idea of the multiple factors whose interaction produces the revolutionary situation. Such situation is termed by Hegopian as 'antecedent condition'.[24] W.F. Werthein raised some questions against the theory of revolution of Marx and Lenin. He wrote, "Is there any uniformity to be discovered in the manifold situations throughout the world history which we can assess, by hindsight, as pre-revolutionary".[25] In addition to this he raised many issues: whether revolutions occur in situation of extreme misery or under conditions of economic growth, whether revolutions appear under political conditions of extreme harshness or under regimes where political control has been somewhat relaxed and consequently, the dissatisfied groups enjoy some latitude for non occurring.[25] With this observation he was of the view that there would be a separate influence and impact according to the different historical period in which a revolution occurs.

An American researcher James G. Davies, wrote, "revolution usually occurs not when the hardship and privation are at their worst but when periods of improvement and progress, which have bred optimism and hope, give way to sudden and rapid decline. This is when discontent flows over a consequence of profound disappointment and collapse of hope."[27] He is of the opinion that revolution is engendered neither by poverty nor by satiety but by real situation in which social progress is not as rapid as has been expected. William J. Pomeroy thinks that "revolutions are not created by the reading of manifestoes in a village street, but are produced by deep seated basic social condition".[28] He further said that people are ready for struggle when their conditions of life are comparatively worsen, when they have a clear aim and when they are organized into a force. Thus various writers and social scientists of both Marxist and non-Marxist schools of thought advanced different theories about the causes of the outbreak of revolution. Whatever the case may be it is also an undeniable fact that the maximum degree of anger of the people, the dissatisfaction and unhappiness of the masses broke out only when their normal economic life is seriously disturbed either by the exploiter group of the existing society or imperialist force. Walter Laquir has rightly observed that the incident that sparks a revolution may be trivial but temporary economic crisis have played a certain part in the outbreak of revolution. But Wolfenstien gave a total different picture about the causes of the outbreak of the revolution. Apart from the social, economic and other aspects he also tried to point out the intention and desire of the revolutionary actors of the society. He was of the view that in the modern revolutionary movement the role of the leadership is the predominant factor for the outbreak of the revolution. After making an extensive observation and analysis of revolution and reason for the outbreak of revolution he came to the conclusion that revolution is a politics of repeat and violent social change "either because the society is already in the throes of upheavals or because the revolutionary actors desire political power in order to make a sweeping change in every nature of the society."[29]

**Classification of Revolutionary Movements**

The character and nature of the revolutionary movements are not at all identical or almost all the same. Some important contibutors to this concept of the typology of the revolutionary movements are Feliks Gross, George Peter, E. Victor Wolfenstien, Paul Wilknson, etc. According to Feliks Gross there are four types of revolutions i.e., 1. Revolution from the bottom, 2. Revolution from the top, 3 Combined seizure of power, and 4. Palace revolution.

Revolution from the bottom as characterized by Felis Gross, is a large spontaneous mass movement, which erupts a suddn explosion and affects the whole life of the society and forcing the ne' leadership to agree to the introduction of far reaching political and scial reform.

Revolution from the top means the seizure of power by an armed group of men who seize the power at pinnacle. Such type of revolution according to Feliks, is organized and planned as opposed to spontaneous mass movement. Their only aim is to capture the government and they have no wish to introduce social cange.

Combined seizure of power is a form of revolution in which the revolutionary actors from the top combined with a limitd revolution from the bottom. Feliks Gross said in such cases, the cəture of the political and governmental apparatus is accompanied by a movement of the broad masses.

Palace revolution as characterized by Feliks means a shift in the distribution of power within the ruling super elite. Sometimes it is also associated with violence. In such revolution a dissident group within the elite not by an outside group carries out the seizure of power. He further said that such type of revolutionaries does not champion political or social change.[30]

George Peter in his 'The Process of Revolution' further developed the idea of classification of Feliks. He did not make any drastic departure from the typology of Feliks. He categorized the revolutionary movement into five different types i.e., 1. A great national revolution, 2. Coup d'etate, 3. Palace revolution, 4. Insurrection, and 5. Revolution of system. The first three categories are almost all the same with the classification of Feliks. His concept of a great national revolution may be equated with Feliks' idea of revolution from the bottom, the coup d'etate with Feliks' idea of revolution from the top and the palace revolution. But the last two categories are new ideas of the typology of the revolutionary movement. George Peter defined 'insurrection' as revolt against unjust administration, law or government; 'revolution of system' means to describe the most extensive social change including that of entire social system. He also described it as great historical changes which include transition from city-state to empire; from empire to feudal system and from feudal system to nation state.

The nature of the classification of revolutionary movements of Feliks and Peter was observed by the Marxian writers as a serious ignorance of the social and economic aspects of the revolutionary process. They are of the view that the type of the characterization of the nature of the revolution by the western writers contains no analysis of the social and economic genesis of the revolution nor its class character. According to them the analysis of the western writers is restricted to the study of the power struggle between elites. So their nature of classification is superficial and one sided.[32] In regard to the criteria of classification of revolution R. Tanter and M. Middlarsky introduced four aspects: 1. The degree of mass participation, 2. The length of the revolutionary process, 3. The level of violence, and 4. Goals of the insurgents. The idea given by the two writers is not original. They are of the view that this concept has a great deal in common with that evolved by Feliks Gross and George Peter. Therefore the classification of Tanter and Middlarsky is regarded as the typical example of subjectivist and most unexpected combination of heterogeneous elements.[33] At the same time their theory of the classification of the types of revolution based on the basis of these four points mentioned above by bringing together all the unconnected criteria as the degree of popular participation in a revolution and its duration was also regarded as an illegitimate attempt.

Another western writer Mostafa Rejai made another attempt to define the political revolution by adding an additional criterion. His theory was based on the principle of the criterion of target. He wrote, "The typology offered below is based upon a single criterion: the target or targets of political revolution. The target, or 'enemy' against which a political revolution is directed is the most distinctive characteristic."[34] By employing the criterion of target M. Rejai tried to identify three types of political revolution i.e. civil revolution, national revolution and abortive revolution. Violent overthrow of a domestic enemy by the masses, the replacement of one political regime by another and to introduce overall social change belong to the category of civil revolution. He also said that the term 'civil' simply suggests that the target of political revolution is an internal one and so a civil revolution is not the same as a civil war. The 'national revolution' means the mass violent overthrow of a foreign (external) power, a change in the political system, the termination of foreign rule, and the institutionalization of social change. From his conceptual idea it can be presumed that the national revolution might be spearheaded against the puppet regimes. Rejai had categorically stated that the definition of a national revolution is similar to that of a revolutionary war. He wrote, "It is in fact both a war and a revolution unfolding at the same time a war because of the formal armed clash involving a foreign government, a revolution because of the mass violence aimed at the internal political and social change."[35] The concept of the 'abortive revolution' as defined by Rejai "refers to the failure of the violent mass movement to reach its target, whether internal or external. Reason may include inept leadership, inadequate organization, failure of communication or planning, suppression at the hands of the authorities. An abortive revolution may be either civil or national."[36]

Like other social scientist Paul Wilkinson also defined the types of revolution into six categories i.e., 1. Revolutionary conspiracies of secret societies, 2. Leninist strategy of revolution, 3. Mass revolutionism, 4. Fascist movement, 5. Totalitarian movement, and 6. Guerrilla based revolution.

The revolutionary conspiracies of secret societies, as defined by Wilkinson, is a type of revolutionary movement launched by a notable and handful group of powerful military officers or ministers in order to seize the control over the organ of government at the top. Such type of revolution does not encourage and welcome the involvement of the masses. Indeed, it is almost the polar opposite to the mass uprising. Wilkinson says this type of revolution is still very much effective in those countries where there is an ineffective regime. In this respect he cited the example of some countries in South America, Central Africa and Middle East. In regard to the characteristic feature of those conspiratorial societies, he wrote, "First, their stress on the exclusiveness of their societies, and members had a duty to infiltrate and influence other organizations, acting as agents of their own brotherhood. Third, it was the aim of these movements to establish small dedicated cadres which would be in a position to take advantage of revolutionary turbulence by stimulating armed rising, and possibly by seizing political control for the brotherhood".[37] He further said that these conspiratorial societies tried to intimate each other, and they often underwent considerable rationalization and modernization before developing into mass revolutionary parties or movements.

The Leninist strategy of revolution, according to Wilkinson was based on three basic and major elements. First, his implacable hostilities towards the whole politico-economic structure of the autocratic government particularly of Russia, and towards the global capitalist system. Second, his maximum degree of awareness of the popular grievances of the masses of peasants and demoralized condition of the industrial worker particularly of the pre-revolutionary period of Russia. Third, his awareness that the democratic mass parties and trade unions of the social democrat model were unwieldy and ideologically and organizationally amorphous to provide a determined, ruthless revolutionary instrument for seizing political power.[39] On the basic understanding of these three points, Lenin strongly asserted to have a party which could take the role of vanguard for a successful socialist revolution. The party, according to Lenin, should be formed by the elements that can maintain strict discipline, absolute loyalty and absolute obedience to the order of the leadership and unfearing dedication to the aim of capturing power. Lenin never tried to compromise his revolutionary principles. He clearly spelt out his uncompromising model of the revolutionary movement in the monograph 'what is to be done'? Here he categorically stated that no revolutionary movement could endure without a stable organization of leaders that maintains continuity. So, he strongly emphasized the need for a solid organization to be constituted mainly by the people professionally engaged in revolutionary activity. Paul Wilkinson pointed out that "Lenin's conception of the exclusive, disciplined, professional revolutionary organization under strict centralized control stems directly, therefore, from the tradition of the conspiratorial secret society. He saw such an organization as something essentially distinct from, and superior to, the mass revolutionary movement."[40] The idea of a centralized party for a successful mass revolution and movement was a unique characteristic feature of the 'Leninist strategy of revolution.' According to Lenin the party organization should be a vital activator, co-coordinator and manipulator of anti-political grievances. He also strongly believed that the party, with its self-professed monopoly of truth about the past, present and future of the revolution, would be able to induce from the above prerequisite mass revolutionary consciousness. The authoritative and comprehensive party ideology is the immediate necessity of the organization. Therefore the organizational activities of the party and mass movement were the secret of the vital success of the Leninist strategy of revolution.

A wide range of racial, students and non-Marxist movements was defined by Paul Wilkinson as an important feature of 'mass revolutionism.' His framework of categorization was based on the principle of the formulation of Stokely Cornichael and Charles Hamilton's ideology of 'liberation for the Black people' against the existing 'system' which they disgusted as racist society and they strongly called for the destruction of the 'system'. In order to achieve their wishes they make an attempt to create a 'new consciousness' among the 'Black people' and coined a new language of struggle and usage of 'liberation'. Cornichael and Charles Hamilton said that they pursued their fellow Negroes to wake up because a revolutionary situation had developed for them to end their social problem. They further mentioned that this is a desperate attempt for Negroes in America and to get their wishes they even prepared to risk violence and to make thinly veiled threat of violence and revenge. They wrote, "Sin the end, we cannot and shall not offer any guarantee that Black power, if achieved, would be non-racist... The final truth is that the white society is not entitled to reassurances even if it were possible to offer them."[41] It is also mentioned that the style of the principle of mass revolutionism has got every possibilities to change its colour if there is no counterbalancing leadership. Paul Wilkinson wrote, "Mass revolutionism that fail to develop any counterbalancing able leadership or organizational centre frequently run out of control. They may lapse into myriad sectarian conflicts and rivalries. Alternatively, unless suppressed, they can develop a momentum of purge, counter purge and general turbulences and dislocation. Sufficient totally to disrupt normal conditions of life, production and administration."[42] To support his observation on the characteristic feature of mass revolutionism he also cited the example of the excess of the Red Guards, Whom Marx himself had stimulated into action in the Chinese Great Protectoral Revolution, 1956–69 that the Peoples Liberation Army had to be called in to provide some guarantee to protection of the dislocated party bureaucracy and to facilitate as return to minimal economic and political stability. So, he further said that "Overestimated mass revolutionism can reach level of a collective psychic disorder with extremely damaging social consequences."

The Fascism, which is regarded by the Marxists as a political principle of 'blood thirsty, terrorist dictatorship of the most reactionary, chauvinistic and aggressive factor of the exploiting classes, engendered by the general crisis of competition'"[43] is treated by Paul Wilkinson as one of the important type of revolutionary movements. Fascism appeared in the early 1920s as a reaction to the world economic and political crisis. Soon after it turned into a vehement and dangerous enemy of all progressive mankind, above all, of the international workers' movement. On the other hand, Fascist movement started by Mussolini in Italy during the 1920s had acquired some ideas and slogans, which were very much popular among the people who were affected by the post war disillusion and the poverty of the depression.

The main objective of the Italian Fascist movement was to shake off the constraints of bourgeois liberal democratic value and practices, to give more emphasis on the industrial growth and modernization, to exalt the role of the youth. On the other hand, Mussolini who started his political career as a socialist party organizer and propagandist had successfully led the movement by using the technique of the mass movement. In order to consolidate his personal charisma and political power as dictator he utilized all the paraphernalia of youth movement, used the symbolism and ritual of military organization and manipulative activities was also adopted in the role of the Italian Fascism and the character of German Fascism, Marxist of Nazism. Italian Fascism lacked the racialist ideology, which Hitler successfully used in his revolutionary movement. On the basis of this ideology Hitler successfully prepared mass revolutionist strategies, mass propaganda and party organization. Another great achievement of Hitler was his successful appeal to the German youths to extend their help to revenge against the humiliation imposed by the Versailles powers. Paul Wilkinson said that Fascism was to some extent a revolution that "it was ultra-patriotic, ultra-nationalist and pro-militarist in policy and style."[44]

Totalitarian movement is also classified as another type of revolutionary movement. The term 'totalitarian' is defined by Marxist writers as 'a social political system characterized by the all embracing despotic interventions of the authoritarian bureaucratic state in the life of society and individual."[45] The main feature of the principle of 'totalitarianism' is to make a calculated destruction of all rival parties, loyalties and potential bases of opposition to accomplish revolutionary seizure of power. Another effective aspect of the 'totalitarian movement' was that for the purpose of acquiring popular legitimization and support the leader of the movement always gave motivation to all the people of different class of the society at a high level with a view to keep their allegiance and commitment to the regime. It is also mentioned that the totalitarian state was to maintain the strict control and surveillance over the movement, their youths, workers, peasants and even the cultural life. To achieve more effective support and to maintain loyalty to the regime the leaders put special attention to propaganda dissemination and made heavy investment in mass indoctrination specially the youths. The totalitarian regimes give too much emphasis on this policy because the leaders fully know that this is the best form of psychological and ideological defence against the anti-totalitarian regime and external forces. Wilkinson observed that this policy is vital to prepare successive generations for the possibility of military service for the regime. The Marxian writers said that the true character of totalitarian feature is observed in the absolute monarchies, for example Bonapartist regime of 19th century and similar regimes in Germany, Italy, Chile, etc. in the 20th century. The totalitarian regimes of these areas make an attempt to slander the social system in the socialist countries by ignoring the true democratic issue of the reform taking place in these countries. Paul Wilkinson wrote, "the mass movement basis to totalitarian is, therefore, the essential means by which the totalitarian nation is welded together, and to the regime, it is the creator of the will which enable the regimes to survive."[46]. Indeed, the totalitarian movements got its strength and inspiration from its method of sustaining ideological commitment, in communicating the charisma and charismatic symbol of revolution participation in the party and its satellite organization among the youths.

Guerrilla-based revolution is also classified by Wilkinson as one of the important types of revolutionary movements. From the context of the present revolutionary concept, it can be suggested that this type of revolution, because of its highly scientific techniques which can establish a firm foundation of support among the rural and urban population, has become the most successful operation in modern revolutionary movement. It is also an accepted view among the social scientists that the use of armed revolutionary struggle for independence from any type of administration or social structure is an important part of historical development. And people usually used armed method of revolution only when their non-violent attempt was exhausted and after being provoked into it. Wilkinson has rightly pointed out that the ability to establish a firm foundation of popular support among the poor is the strength of modern revolutionary movement and this base is vital to the successful operation of guerrilla revolution[47]. W.J. Pomeroy also expressed his observation on the same line. He said that "the occurrence of armed revolutionary struggle throughout this present period in many sectors of the world, in its guerrilla form or in other forms, can be traced in every case to a denial by imperialist or by pro imperialist government, of peaceful means for the masses of people to gain national aims, including direct armed intervention to reverse a popular trend towards independence".[48] This type of revolutionary movement uses violence against violence. This is the only alternative means for those people who faced the military suppression and counter revolutionary warfare. From the evidences of the modern revolutionary movement it can be said that the guerrilla based revolutionary movement is the most effective means for an initially unarmed people to struggle against suppression. So it has greatly expanded its popular application to the present period. Here W.J. Pomeroy pointed out the differences between the guerrilla warfare which occurred in other historical periods and guerrilla warfare as a form of revolutionary struggle. The guerrilla warfare as the form of revolutionary struggle has possessed certain characteristic features of qualification such as. broad mass base, highly organized structure with democratic character and enjoy the support of anti-imperialist population. But the form of guerrilla activity without a revolutionary aim and revolutionary participation of masses has led to the degeneration in brigandage. According to Lenin the people who take up arms in the initial stages of popular guerrilla struggle are not 'a minority of agitators.' Rather they are the more advanced, more militant and more decisive elements of a revolutionized people. With regard to the importance of the guerrilla based revolutionary movement in the present context of the freedom struggle, Wilkinson has rightly observed that this base is vital to the successful operation of revolutionary movement. He wrote, "... it ensures, because of its entirely autonomous character, the vital supply of manpower, aid and succour, and invaluable secure retreats and weapons dumps."[49] Mao-Tse-Tung also gave an elaborate explanation about the nature and strategy of the guerrilla based revolution. At the end he emphasized the massive support of the masses for the successful operation of guerrilla based revolutionary movement. He said that the most important victory is to use the people so that guerrilla force should establish an invincible base of mass support. Thus most of the observations about the characteristic feature of guerrilla based revolutionary movement were based on the support of the masses. Nobody mentioned about the ideological principle of the guerrilla warfare. Even Che Guevara who was a staunch ideologue of the principle of Marxism said that the successful combat of guerrilla based revolutionary movement depends entirely on "constant mobility, constant distrust and constant vigilance'. In this respect it is suggested that for an effective guerrilla based revolutionary movement a clear cut ideology and an elaborate set of revolutionary principles or doctrines is not a pre-requisite one.[50]

The doctrines and policies of guerrilla based revolutionary movement, both before and after seizure of power, are more genuinely moulded by the whims and declarations of their charismatic leaders.[51] All the writers' directly or indirectly mentioned about the basic character of the guerrilla based revolutionary movement on the basis of the importance of mass support and integrity of the leadership. Col. CM. Woodhouse, a British theoretician of guerrilla warfare said. "There has never been a successful guerrilla war conducted in an area where the populace is hostile to the guerrillas, and conversely it is impossible to stamp out a guerrilla war in an area where populace continues to support the guerrillas". Indeed, the relation of guerrillas to population is the key to an understanding of struggle for national liberation. Therefore guerrilla warfare, as observed by Pomeroy "is a type of warfare demanding determined, disciplined and uncompromising leadership, within the context of popular democracy".[52]

Thus different writers of both Marxian and non-Marxian thought of schools advanced different theories on revolution on the basis of their observations. But one thing is clear from these theories that revolution is a form of politics to bring a radical change in the existing order by using violent method. And in regard to the causes of that outbreak of the revolutionary movement, Wolfenstein said that "the revolution broke out either because the society is already in the throes of upheavals or because the revolutionary actors desire political power in order to make a sweeping change in the very nature of the society."[53]

## REVOLUTIONARY MOVEMENTS IN THE PRE-MERGER MANIPUR

Right from the early historical periods the people of Manipur had an opportunity to enjoy a very good experience of the activities of the revolutionary movements, which broke out in the different phases of the history of this place. However, most of the revolutionary movements of the early period were dominated by palace revolt, which is a type of revolution as classified by Gross Feliks. So there was no concrete evidence about the nature of the revolution, which was based on the social and economic issues of the country. The whole character of almost all the movements was focused on the shifting of power from one ruling elite group to another group of the same class. Therefore, the involvement and participation of the masses was not figured in the chronicles and other literary sources of the history of this place. As a result of this the outcome of the movement and its impact was concentrated and confined only to limited areas with a limited scope. However, in the last part of the 19th and the middle of the 20th century the people again witnessed the activities of the two important revolutionary movements which rendered a significant impact in the future history of Manipur. The first one was the 'revolutionary movement of 1890' and another was the armed 'revolutionary movement of 1948-51'.

**REVOLT OF 1890**

The Revolt of 1890 which broke out just after the establishments of relationship between Manipur and British was a great landmark in the history of this state. Though, it was confined with a limited scope and objective, the result of this movement had produced a significant impact in the future history of this state. No doubt like other revolutionary movements the basic character of the movement was to make an attempt to control the political and administrative power of the state by a group of ruling elite group. In the history of this state it is popularly known as the 'Revolt of 1890.' The historical background of the causes for the outbreak of this revolt was more or less directly related with the internal feuds between the two groups of princes. They were all the sons of late Maharaja Chandrakriti Singh. Surchandra Singh, the Maharaja of Manipur was the leader of one group. The other members of this group were Pakka Sana alias Bhairabjit, Keshwarjit, Gopal Sana alias Padmalochand and another group was led by Kullachandra Singh. Yuvaraj or crown prince of the state. Other members were Tikendrajit alias Koireng, Angousana Singh and Zillangamba Singh. The main actor of the revolution was Tikendrajit Singh. There might have been many factors for their internal conflict but the final outburst was made on the 21st September 1890. On this very day the group led by Kullachandra attacked the royal palace and captured the administrative power by removing the group of Surchandra Singh. It is quite obvious that the objective of the revolt never asked for any type of changes in the political system and social order of the state. The only objective was to control the administrative power. The character of the movement was purely on the line of the palace revolt as categorized by Feliks in his classification of the revolutionary movement. The attempt to shift in the distribution of power within the ruling elite is the main characteristic feature of this type of revolutionary movement. The revolt of 1890 was a violent type of movement. One group acquired the political power not in the process of a peaceful way. This was also another feature of the palace revolt. Feliks has rightly said that the association of violent means for the capture of power was also another feature of this type of revolutionary movement.

The importance of this revolutionary movement lies not in the course of their action but on the impact of the post-revolutionary period. It is a fact that just after the removal from the chair of power Surchandra made a serious attempt to get back the political power again with the help of the British. Ultimately such type of approach gave the golden opportunity to the British to interfere in the domestic affairs of the independence Manipur State. Though many questions were raised on the legal and moral authority of the British in their successful attempt to interfere in the affairs of the state, their direct involvement finally led to the outbreak of Anglo-Manipur War of 1891. In that war Manipur was defeated and British occupied it on the 27th April 1891. This war produced two important results, establishment of the direct colonial administration in Manipur and the loss of the distinctive national identity of the people of Manipur.

With regard to the establishment of direct British rule over Manipur, right from the very beginning the British authority had a strong desire to extend their imperialist hand in Manipur as they took Manipur as a strategic place both from political and commercial point of view. This idea was clearly shown in the nature of the signing of the Treaty of 1762 between Manipur and British. But they were compelled by the existing political scenario of the surrounding areas of Southeast Asia not to exercise their natural policy very soon. Again in the year 1826 the British got another opportunity to implement their policy. In 1826 Manipur was liberated from the hands of Burma with the full military support of the British. In the international treaty signed at Yandaboo between British and Burma, the independence of Manipur was recognized by both powers. This time also if the British had a strong desire, they could have done it very easily. But British fully realized the problems, which they were supposed to face if they establish their direct administration in Manipur. To keep Manipur as a buffer state between British and Burma was an immediate necessity of that time. Therefore Manipur was made buffer state for the benefit of the British. In the meantime the British were able to control the whole areas of Southeast Asian countries. Almost all the areas of India up to Assam to the east was under the direct administration of the British and just after the end of Third Anglo Burmese War in the year 1885 all the area of Burma was under the control of the British. Therefore after this political development the position of Manipur as a 'buffer state' was no longer required to the British. They were waiting for an opportunity to establish their direct administration. That opportunity was given by the revolt of 1890. The moment they got the opportunity the British immediately occupied Manipur in 1891.

The occupation of Manipur and establishment of direct British rule means the end of the political status of a sovereign independent state which the people enjoyed from the early historical period with a distinctive national identity. Then after the introduction of colonial administration of British the people began to survive as a second-class citizen in their own motherland. Thus for a long period of time i.e. from 1891 to 1947 the people of Manipur had witnessed a series of political developments which greatly injured their national identity. During this period the people got the experience of the outbreak of different types of anti-imperialist and anti-feudal movement which challenged the authoritarian character of these two institutions. The indirect objective of these movements was more or less concerned with preservation and maintenance of the distinctive identity of the Manipuri people. Gradually the idea of political consciousness was developed among the people in the first part of the 20th century. And the people began to ask to remove the colonial and feudal administrative system and they made a proposal to replace it by a political system based on the principle of democracy. But two groups of people emerged. One group was in favour of the establishment of separate political identity of Manipur and another group was not in favour of this proposal. The element of the latter group was highly influenced by the Indianite political character and so they openly expressed their desire to make Manipur a part of India. Majority of the elite people of the state of that period were in favour of integration of Manipur into India. So with a strong influence and initiative of these people Manipur finally became a part of India on the 15th October 1949 and distinctive political character of Manipur state was completely lost. And along with this a distinctive separate identity of the people of Manipur was also completely vanished. This is the ultimate result of the revolt of 1890.

## ARMED REVOLUTIONARY MOVEMENTS, 1948-51

The outbreak of armed revolutionary movement in the year 1948 was another form of revolutionary movement in the history of the pre-merger period of Manipur. This movement was launched under the dynamic leadership of Hijam Irabot Singh with an objective for the establishment of a separate political identity of Manipur based on a classless society by removing feudal and imperialist force.

The revolutionary movement of Hijam Irabot Singh was an outcome of his long struggle based on non-violent agitation for the upliftment of the social, economic and political condition of the people. He started his revolutionary career as social and religious activities under the banner of the Nikhil Hindu Manipuri Mahasabha. During this period he threw many challenges in democratic way against the social and religious policies adopted by the feudal and colonial administrators. Apart from this he also tried to bring all the Manipuri people who were scattered in different areas outside Manipur under the banner of certain concrete understanding. His strong desire was clearly reflected in his speech at the Mandalay session of the Nikhil Hindu Manipuri Mahasabha. He was also fully aware that without a political struggle things would not come to a right direction. Therefore on the 4th session of the Mahasabha which was known popularly as 'Chinga Session' of 1938, the Mahasabha became a political party. The name also changed to 'Nikhil Manipuri Mahasabha'. This was a big jump on his non-violent type of revolutionary movement. Through the political platform of Nikhil Manipuri Mahasabha, Irabot Singh began to take up many political issues which greatly helped to the growth of political consciousness among the common people of Manipur. The demand for the establishment of a responsible government and the amalgamation of the administration of hills and plains under a single administrative unit laid a very good foundation for the growth of an idea of political institution and unity among the different groups of people within the social and political framework of Manipuri nationalism. Thus under his leadership a long political and social democratic revolution was launched by the people particularly the people of rural areas of Manipur.

However, Irabot was not free from many obstacles. A big problem was the issue of the political elements in the state who were greatly influenced by the Indianite political colour and concept. Their main objective was to make Manipur become a part of India, so that there would be peace and development in the state. Taking the opportunity of this situation some outside forces made a strong proposal to form a separate state called 'Purbanchal State' which was to be constituted of Manipur, Lushai and Tripura. This idea was supported by some forceful political elements in Manipur. Irabot was not in favour of this proposal. His only desire was to maintain a distinctive identity of Manipur state and her people. To make a strong protest against this move he prepared for a big gathering of the masses on 21st September 1948 at the hall of Manipur Dramatic Union (MDU) of Imphal. But unfortunately some undesirable incidents occurred during the process of organization of the meeting at Pungdongbam village where one police officer was killed by the mob. The government alleged that it was the work of the members of the party of Irabot. Thus, this situation compelled him to go to underground activities for the fulfillment of his political and social aim. Indeed this incident was a turning point in his political career. Then from non-violence he changed his method of political movement to armed-uprising. His armed revolution continued till his death in the year 1951.

Like the revolt of 1890, the importance of the armed revolutionary movement of 1948 lies in the outcome of its movement. The biggest positive impact of the revolution was its successful efforts for the growth and consolidation of the idea of oneness among the Manipuri people. The basic aim of Irabot was to bring unity among the Manipuris who inhabited in other areas outside Manipur. He also strongly asserted that Manipuris should have the privilege to enjoy the opportunity and right to develop and maintain their culture, politics and social order etc. He clearly mentioned these aspects in his different political platform right from the time of Nikhil Hindu Manipuri Mahasabha. He also gave too much importance to the decision of the people. He always said that the question of preservation of national identity of Manipur should be left to the decision of the people. He was not in favour of the integration of Manipur with India. Chhatradhani who was a close associate of Irabot observes that the moment he received the information of the signing of Merger Agreement by the Maharaja, who was a constitutional head, he expressed that the Maharaja could not do it without the comment of the people,[54] but some writers strongly refuted this view. According to these writers Irabot never had any opinion against the integration of Manipur into India. Whatever the opinion may be the activities of his revolutionary movement are to be analyzed critically as a whole his revolutionary movement left a profound impact on political and social life of the people of the state which ultimately led to the growth of the revolutionary ideas among the younger generations. His revolutionary ideas and action gave a strong influence to the young people to reassert their strong claim for the establishment of a separate political and national identity of Manipuri people. From this point of view in one way or other Hijam Irabot Singh may be regarded as the founding father of the growth of idea of Manipuri nationalism among the people and his revolutionary movement laid the foundation for the growth of a series of revolutionary activities in the future historical process of Manipur. Therefore, because of his positive political activities R. Constantine regarded Irabot as a "national leadership timbre'.[55]

## NOTES

1. Roy, Sibnarary. *For a Revolutionary from Below*. India: Minerva. P. 127.
2. Ibid.
3. Martin, E. D. 1920. *The Behaviour of Crowds: A Psychological Study*. New York. P. 184.
4. Ellwood, Charles A. 1920. *Sociology in its Psychological Aspects*. New York. P. 163.
5. Garlin, M & L. Kazakova. 1980. *Elitist Revolution or Revolution of the Masses*. Moscow. P.12.

6. Arrendt. Hannah. 1963. *On Revolution*. New York. P. 13.

7. Cheng. Ronald Yena-Lin. Ed 1993.*The Sociology of Revolution: Reading on Political Upheavals and Popular Unrest*. Chicago. P.2.

8. Hegopian. Mark N. *Regimes, Movements and Ideologies: A Comparative Introduction to Political Science*. New York

9. Cohan. A.S. 1975. *Theories of Revolution: An Introduction*. University of Lancaster P.11.

10. Hegopian. Mark N. Op. cit. P. 276.

11. Garlin M. & L. Kazakova. Op.cit. P 13.

12. Batalov, E. 1983. *Lenins Theory on Revolution*. Moscow: Progress Publisher. P.9.

13. Ibid.

14. Lenin. V.I. 1973. *Collected Works*. Vol. 33. Moscow. P. 110.

15. Lenin. V.I. 1973. *Collected Works*. Vol. 26. Moscow. P. 439.

16. Petter, George Sawyer. 1971.*The Process of Revolution*. P.3.

17. Wolfenstien, E. Victor. 1971. *The Revolutionary Personality, Lenin, Trotsky, Gandhi*. New Jersey, U.S.A. P. 20.

18. *Encyclopedia of Social Science*.Vol.13-14. P. 501.

19. Lenin, V.I. *Collected Works*. Vol.21. Pp. 213-14.

20. Prof. Sergei and P. Novoslov. 1981. *Problems of the Communist Movement*. Moscow.P.116.

21. Lenin, V.I. *Collected Works*. Vol. 21. P. 451.

22. Ibid. P.214.

23. Hagopian. Mark. Op.Cit. P. 285.

24. Ibid.

25. W.F. Wetheim. 1974. *Revolution: The Rising Waves of Emancipation*. London. P. 181.

26. Ibid.

27. M. Garlin and L. Kazekova Op. cit. P. 58.

28. Pomeroy, William J. *Guerrilla and Counter Guerrilla Warfare*. P. 51.

29. Folfenstien, E. Victor. Op.cit. P. 20.

30. Gross, Feliks. 1958. *The Seizure of Political Powers in a Century and Revolution*. New York. Pp. 39, 47, 52, 54.

31. Petter. George. 1971. *The Process of Revolution*. New York. P. 3.

32. Garlin, M. and L. Kazokova. Op.cit. P. 39.

33. Garlin, M. and L. Kazokova. Ibid. P. 40.

34. Rejai, M. 1973. *The Strategy of Political Revolution*. New York. Pp. 19-20.
35. Rejai. M. Ibid. P. 20.
36. Rejai, M. Ibid.
37. Wilkinson, Paul. 1971. *Social Movements*.P. 140.
38. Ibid.
39. Ibid. P. 141.
40. Ibid. P. 143.
41. Cainmichael, S. and C. Hamilton. 1968. *Black Power*. London P.49. (Quoted in *Social Movements*. Ibid. P. 145).
42. Wilkinson, Paul. Op. cit. P. 146.
43. *Dictionary of Phiiosophy*. Progress Publisher. 1984. P. 90.
44. Wilkinson, Paul. Op. cit. P. 149.
45. *Dictionary of Philosophy*. Op.cit. 1984. P. 426.
46. Wilkinson, Paul. Op. cit. P. 149.
47. Wilkinson, Paul. Ibid. P. 137.
48. Pomeroy, William J. Op. cit. P. 14.
49. Wilkinson, Paul. Op. cit. P. 138.
50. Wilkinson, Paul. Ibid. P. 139.
51. Wilkinson, Paul. Ibid.
52. Pomeroy, William J. Op. cit. P. 97.
53. Wolfenstein, E. Victor. Op. cit. P. 20
54. Chhatradhary, S. 1977. *Manipur Itihasta Irabot*. P.69. Op. cit. P. 20.
55. Contenstine, R. 1981. *Manipur: Maid of the Mountain*. P.235.

## CHAPTER TWO

# GENESIS OF THE MOVEMENTS

The outbreak of different types of social movements is not a new phenomenon in the history of modern Manipur. Professor Gangmumei has rightly observed that "revolutions and rebellions occurred in Manipur in the $20^{th}$ century at almost regular intervals".[1] Right from the beginning of the colonial rule, from the First Women Agitation of 1904, the people of the state began to witness series of different types of social movements which always played a vital role with a great significant impact on every aspects of the social, economic and political life of the people. However, since these movements had limited aim and objective, they were not able to come up to the level of a revolutionary movement. The basic objective of these movements was to improve the economic and administrative conditions of the state. They never attacked the basic foundation of the evils of the social order which is the prerequisite factor for any type of revolution. Therefore, these movements as a whole, may be treated as actions and attempts of a body of persons for a particular objective.

Just after the integration of the state into India, the people again witnessed the outbreak of a series of armed revolutionary movements which strongly emphasised the establishment of a separate political identity of Manipur. And the outbreak of such type of revolutionary movement has assumed predominant feature in the history of the post-merger Manipur. In this respect it is observed that the present movements, though they are not a direct continuation of the early movements, their historical roots engrained in them.[2] The growing idea and emergence of the concept of Manipuri nationalism was also another feature of the outbreak of these movements. This ideological concept was the motivating factor for the emergence of the idea of oneness among the people of this state. Whatever the case may be, the outbreak of such type of movements have produced a significant impact on the political development of the state.

The movement for the attainment of a full fledged state by the Manipur National Union in the early 1950s may be observed as the beginning of the plantation of the idea of revolutionary movements in Manipur. To an answer of a question, one of the most prominent ex-revolutionary leader of a party had categorically stated that the dissatisfaction with the attitude of the Indian Government, discontentment among the educated people, the issue of the merger of Manipur to India, the economic exploitation by the Mayangs (foreigners), etc. were the main factors for the outbreak of the armed revolutionary movement. Another ex-revolutionary leader said that the lost pride and glory of the political status of this state could be restored only by an armed revolutionary movement. They strongly asserted that Manipur was integrated into Indian Union in a most uncivilized and undemocratic way. They accused the Indian Government for adopting the principles of neo-colonialism. They all believed that the merger of Manipur into India was nothing but to create a ground for the burial of the identity of the indigenous people of the state. Therefore, the integration of Manipur into India was the motive force for the starting of revolutionary movement in this state. In this respect we may analyse some historical facts and events of the pre- and post- merger period, which may be treated as important factors for the growth of discontentment among the people of the state.

## POLITICAL

On the 15th of August, 1947 the British left Manipur. Accordingly she regained her independence. And the relationship between India and Manipur was established through an office of the 'Dominion Agent'. On the other hand the establishment of the office of Dominion Agent in Manipur itself may be taken as mark of the beginning of the losing of the political identity of this state. It is said that through this office the Government of India was able to interfere very effectively in the internal issues of the state.[3] On the other hand, by taking the advantage of this office, the leaders of the Government of India committed a series of calculated encroachments on the independent identity of the political status of Manipur. Although it is not required to go into detail about the history of the procedure of how Manipur was integrated into India, it is quite obvious from the records that right from the beginning, the leaders of India particularly of Congress Party had already married with the concept of imperialism. In a resolution passed on the 15th of June, 1947, the Congress Party openly declared that "they could not admit the right of any state in India to declare its independence to live in isolation from the rest of India"[14]. It was on the basis of the principle of this resolution that the leader of the Congress Party of India made a successful attempt to integrate all the princely states into India. Manipur was also a victim of this policy. In this respect we may analyze the historical process leading to the integration of Manipur into India.

Just after the establishment of Nikhil Manipuri Mahasabha as a political party, the people of Manipur strongly demanded for the abolition of feudal system of administration and strongly emphasized the establishment of a responsible government, which was to be constituted on the basis of the universal adult franchise. The demand was further intensified by the Manipur State Congress which was established on the 4th of October, 1946 at Imphal. Taking advantage of the fluid political situation in the state the Congress leaders of India began to interfere in the internal administration of the state in an indirect way in collusion with the leaders of the State Congress Party. The demand for the establishment of a responsible government in Manipur became very strong and in response to the desire of the people, the State Government enacted a new constitution known as 'Manipur State Constitution' and it was an obligatory to the state to follow the provisions of the Constitution. Some leaders from India had also suggested that the Maharaja of Manipur had to respect the provisions of the new Constitution and asked him not to ignore the provisions of the Constitution.[5] Here we can see the elements of democratic essence in their approach. In the meantime an issue for the appointment of 'Dewan' was raised and it became a serious matter for the State Government. But the position of 'Dewan' was not in the provisions of the Manipur State Constitution. When this issue was raised by the Government of India, the Maharaja tried to convince them by pointing out that since it was not a part of the Constitution he was not in a position to appoint a 'Dewan'. At this stage the Government of India had forgotten their democratic principles and idea and pressed the Maharaja to appoint a 'Dewan' by saying that the Government of India did recognize neither the Manipur State Council nor the State Assembly but the Maharaja only.[6] Such type of political stand of the Government of India was highly uncalled for and at the same time they did not have the legal right to recognize or to de-recognize Manipur State Council because Manipur was not under the Dominion of India. This type of political action was nothing but to make an undeclared aggression against Manipur and they had adopted this policy by taking the advantage of the internal political weakness of Manipur.

When the Maharaja refused to sign the merger agreement the leaders of the Indian Government tried to convince him by saying that the Maharaja might be rest assured that the Government of India would take a complete responsibility in the matters of meeting whatever might be raised by the people of the state.[7] In this connection, the very words of the ideal statement of Pandit Nehru which he delivered in the session of the Constituent Assembly on the 5th of March, 1948 may be recalled. He had strongly stressed that the real integration was not at the top level of government but at the level of the people. He said, "there has been a bringing together of a number of states into the Union of India and certain number of major states remain as separate entities. But what is actually important and if I may say so, even more important is not this integration externally but the inner integration, that is the growth of democratic institution and responsible governments in the states, because that brings about a real integration not at the top level of the government but at the level of the people".[8] V.N. Gadgil, the then Minister of Works and who was also in charge of the Home Minister, also categorically mentioned the value of the opinion of the people of the concerned state. In his official statement in the Constituent Assembly on the 15th of March, 1948 he again mentioned that "there is no desire on our part, in any way to compel or coerce them into merger or integration. If they wish to remain as separate autonomous units, we could have no objection but if the ruler and the people of any of these states desire to merge with the neighbouring state, on a voluntary basis obviously the Government of India cannot say 'no'".[9] On the other hand, when the Maharaja refused to sign the agreement and when the Indian officials sought his advice, Sardar Vallabhbhai

Patel, the Union Home Minister, asked the officials whether there was not a 'Brigadier' in Shillong. Thus there were a lot of contradictory versions among the leading political leaders of the Government of India in respect of their principle on democracy. From these facts the people could see the undemocratic elements in the minds of the leaders of the Indian government, who were regarded to be a staunch supporter of democratic principles. It seems that their concept of democracy was deeply coloured by the imperialist and colonial tendencies which were the remnants of the British policy.

The relegation of the political status of Manipur from the position of a constitutional monarch to that the political unit of the Indian Union was the immediate outcome of the merger. This stage was the most shocking and pitiable political position of Manipur. Before the merger the sizeable educated section of the society thought that the merger of Manipur into India would bring peace and prosperity and there would be a lot of development in every aspects of life of the people. However, just after integration things happened contrary to the expectation of the people. The denial of democratic rights by the Government of India which were enjoyed by the people between 1947-49 was the most important and unforgettable political disaster of this state. It was an irony that the leaders of the Government of India, who claimed to be the upholder of the democratic values, had denied the democratic rights to the minority group of the people just after the integration. The Government had abolished all the democratic institutions and Central Rule with bureaucratic set up was established and the entire administration of Manipur was put in the hands of a single bureaucratic officer. It is also a fact after seeing all these political developments, even the people who strongly advocated for merger into India began to express their dissatisfaction at the attitude of the Indian government. The fact was that the government of India refused to establish a responsible government on the pretext of the lack democratic experience. But their real intention was to destroy the identity of the people. This fact was clearly demonstrated by the recommendation of the State Reorganization Commission. The Commission even went to the extent that Manipur should be merged into Assam and formed a district.[10] It is indeed unfortunate on the part of the leader of the Indian government for their deliberate ignorance of the fact that the people of Manipur had more democratic experience than the rest of the people of India because before merger the people had the experience of the working of legislative assembly which was established on the basis of the universal adult franchise. From these facts the people, particularly the younger generation, felt that the attitude of the Indian government was nothing but to subjugate the indigenous people by showing their military power.

It is also a fact that declaration of the Government of India on the 22[nd] of January, 1950 under which Manipur was put to the political status of a 'Part C' State of the Constitution of India became the most disappointing issue to sensitive educated people of Manipur. They felt that this administrative decision was highly prejudiced and they had taken this decision without giving any chance to reflect their opinion at the time of the passing of the resolution. The fact was that the Constitution of India was formally adopted by the Constitutional Assembly on the 26[th] November, 1949 and India was declared a Republic on 26[th] January, 1950. On the other hand, Manipur was merged into India on the 15[th] of October, 1949. Therefore the integration and the passing of the Constitution occurred almost simultaneously. So it was of the view that if the leaders of the Indian Government really believed in democratic decision they could have given enough chance and scope to the people of Manipur to express their view and opinion because she merged into India before the passing of the Constitution. Thus, political developments in the pre- and post-merger period produced a serious psychological effect on every sensitive educated youth of the state. They also began to express their resentment at the undemocratic attitude of the Indian leaders and after analyzing all sorts of military prepar ation arranged by the officials of Indian Government in and around the areas of the Maharaja of Manipur on the eve of the merger they began to say that Manipur was forcibly taken by the Indian Government to remove their political entity.

Although there were a lot of disappointment and resentment in the growing political trend which was developed after merger, the people of Manipur were quite hopeful that the Indian Government would grant the democratic rights to the people very soon so that they would get an equal political right with the other states of India. To achieve this objective the people had adopted a series of democratic political action and began to demand for a responsible government in Manipur. In this process the people came across a lot of political hindrance which were never expected by them. The movement for establishment of responsible government in Manipur started from the beginning of 1950s. In a memorandum submitted to the Prime Minister of India, the Manipur National Union and Gandhi Sevak Seva strongly asserted that in case the Indian Government failed to give statehood very soon they would start a movement for the creation of a separate buffer state.[11] After this, other political parties also began to demand for a political right. In spite of repeated demand and request the leaders of the Indian Government refused to give any type of political concession to Manipur. On the other hand the members of the State Reorganization Commission made a serious attempt to remove the political entity of this state once for all by recommending that "Manipur should be centrally administered territory for the time being. The ultimate merger of this state in Assam should be kept in view."[12] Although their recommendation was not materialized on the basis of some valid reasons, the motive and integrity of the leaders of the Indian Government was quite exposed. So such type of whimsical political decision of the Indian Government further strengthened the growing separatist tendencies among the people of younger generation. In fact the establishment of a 'Revolutionary Party' by the members of the Manipur National Union might be treated as a great significant step for the emergence of the separatist feeling among the educated youths. The political decision of the Manipur National Union became an eye opener to the government and it became a serious concern to the authority. So to check the growing separatist tendencies leaders like S. Indramani, Yangmaso Shaiza, etc. were kept in jail under Section 151 of Criminal/Procedure Code and Section 124 (A), 153 and 120 (A) of the Indian Penal Code.[13] Although their path of violent activities was not the immediate answer of the people of that time, it had undoubtedly laid a significant foundation for the rapid growth of separatist ideas among the people.

In the meantime, while the movement for the establishment of a responsible government in Manipur was in full swing, another proposal for the formation of Purbanchal State comprising Tripura, Cachar, etc. came into being with a great hope that Congress leaders in Manipur would accept it. It is also mentioned that the Congress leaders both from Tripura and Cachar had pressed the leaders of the Congress Party of Manipur to accept it. In this regard the stand which was taken by the Congress leaders of Manipur was quite praiseworthy. They not only refused to accept it but they also had categorically pointed out that the formation of Purbanchal "will practically be in Bengal State."[14] Therefore they openly declared that Manipur would resist to the last man any move either for merger with Assam or for formation of a state. Such type of political and social entity of this place had strengthened the process of the growth of separatist tendencies among the youths of Manipur. However, the students and youths of that time were quite patient and they believed that the political right of the people would be achieved through democratic means. This was clearly evident from their participation in the movement. At that time the students and youths had taken the leadership role in the demand for the establishment of a responsible government in Manipur. All the people of the hill areas also fully participated in this democratic non-violent approach. The different tribal organizations like the Tangkhul Long, the Paite Union, the Zeilangrong Union, the Kuki National Assembly, etc. had strongly urged the Central Government to establish responsible government in Manipur. In spite of repeated requests from the people, the Government of India refused to grant this rightful democratic demand. Their strong argument was that economically Manipur was not viable to stand alone as a separate state. In this regard the Manipur State Congress Party asserted that so far as the economic matter was concerned, Manipur would not be a burden to the Centre. In a memorandum submitted to the State Reorganization Commission they asserted that "if only the Centre had earnestly taken to the exploration and exploitation of these natural resources", she would become a granary of India.[15] In support of this argument they pointed out the forest resources and other mineral resources as a source for the improvement of the economic position of the state. The main thrust of their argument was that if these available resources were properly explored and systematically utilized, Manipur would be able to stand on its own economic strength. However all sorts of arguments given by the people of Manipur were not acceptable to the Government of India. Such type of negative political stand of the Government of India forced the people of Manipur particularly the younger generation to take a different political attitude against the Government of India. At the same time the people also witnessed the inconsistency in the political principle of the Indian leaders. This inconsistency in their political principles was clearly demonstrated when they dealt with the affairs of the Naga Hills. It is a well-known fact that the people of the Naga Hills were fighting against the Indian Government for the establishment of their own separate political identity. To achieve their goal they adopted the violent means and as a result of this there were a lot of bloodshed between the Indian army and Naga rebels. The Indian Government took a special initiative to bring a solution to the Naga problem. In this respect it can be observed that so far the case of the political movement was concerned there was no sharp differences between Manipur and Naga Hills. Only the basic difference was that Manipur resorted to the non-violent method of democratic principle and Naga people adopted violent method of the principle of armed struggle. But the action and initiative of the Indian leaders in respect of Naga problem have created an impression in the minds of the young people of Manipur that the Indian Government had put enough importance to the armed struggle of Naga people rather than the non-violent principle of the people of Manipur. Their impression was further strengthened when Naga Hills was granted the political status of full-fledged state by the Union Government. Such type of highly partial political attitude of Central Government was taken by the educated youths of the state as a clear indication of the deliberate ignorance of the leaders of the Indian Government to the cause of the non-violent political movement of the people of Manipur. And they also began to be convinced that economic factor was not the criteria for denial of the establishment of a responsible government in Manipur. The granting of statehood to Nagaland was the best example. They felt that comparing the economic viability of Manipur and Nagaland as one of the factors for granting statehood, the former was far better than the latter. Such type of attitude of the leaders of the Indian Government had enraged the people and compelled the educated youth to give up the idea of democratic principle of non-violence. They began to feel that violent method would be the only answer to the political move of the Indian Government. At the same time the extremist elements among the educated youths also began to think that if the democratic rights and privileges enjoyed by their fellow citizens were denied to the people of Manipur, what more things they would be able to get from the association with India. Therefore, the refusal to give the democratic rights to the people of Manipur in time by the Indian Government have laid the basic foundation for the emergence of the separatist tendency among the minds of the educated people of Manipur.

## ECONOMIC

"A population living in abject poverty, lack of employment opportunities occupied with rampant corruption at all levels which is also perhaps the highest on all India level. Disillusionment and dissatisfaction amongst youths which was increasing at an alarming rate. All these factors are potential for the rise of a reserve insurgents." This is the observation of the "Background Paper" of the seminar on Insurgency in Manipur, held on the 9th of September 1989.[16] In this connection Lal Dena observed that "lack of genuine interest in encouraging economic development both on the part of the colonial officials during the British regime and similar lack of interest on the part of Central government in the immediate post-independence period were responsible for the present plight of situation."[17]

It is an accepted view that the economic factor is the most important reason for the growth of any type of movement. People always began to realize their real position only when their economic system was disturbed in a very serious manner. In the case of the North-Eastern India particularly in Manipur, the most important factor for the growth of dissatisfaction among the common people lies in this economic stagnation which creates the idea of separatist tendency among the younger generation. As mentioned above, Manipur had witnessed a series of movements in the pre-independence period and in these movements also economic factor played a major role for the growth of dissatisfaction among the people. An ex-revolutionary leader said that free flow of the trading class from outside the state and their policy of economic exploitation was a great cause for the emergence of the idea of separatist tendencies among the people of Manipur particularly among the educated youths. They said that the present economic policy of the Indian Government in the context of Manipur was nothing but to practice the system of neo-colonialism. In the same way some other ex-revolutionary leaders expressed their discontentment to the economic policy of the Indian Government. They were of the view that the economic policy of the Government of India particularly to Manipur was nothing but to squeeze the economy of the state. Therefore according to them unless some kind of protective measure was adopted the degree of discontentment among the people would be increased tremendously and finally it would lead to the growth of separatist movement among the people. To them the present economic policy of Indian Government in the context of Manipur is exactly the same as it was done by the British in India in pre-independence period. They further said that a state in the grip of neo-colonialism is not the master of its own destiny. From the basis of this argument they believed that so far the economic matter is concerned, Manipur is not the master of her own destiny. The essence of neo-colonialism as observed by Kwane Nkrunah: is that the state which is subject to it is, in theory, independent and has all the outward trapping of international sovereignty. In reality its economic system and thus its political policy is directed from outside."[18] It is an undeniable fact that the change in the shape of the economic position of the state was more or less directly connected with the coming of foreigners from the other countries particularly from the western side. The influx of foreigners may be divided into two waves. The coming of the religious missionaries of Hindu in the beginning of the 18th century may be observed as the first wave of the emergence of foreigners in Manipur. It had produced a far-reaching impact mainly on social life and outlook of the people. However it did not give any type of serious changes in the character of the economic life of the people. The establishment of colonial administration of the British may be taken as the beginning of the second wave of the influx of foreigners in Manipur. The character and nature of the people who were coming to Manipur was totally different from the previous one. They were concerned mainly with the economic life of the state. Their interest in the trade and commerce gave a serious blow to the traditional economic system of Manipur. Ultimately it led to the outbreak of a series of open confrontation against the policy of the colonial government. The blanket protection given by the British to the non-Manipuri traders was the most important reason for the outbreak of the 1939 women's movement. Actually, though the movement was launched by the womenfolk it represented the whole sentiment of the people of the state. Thus the policy of economic exploitation by the non-Manipuri people with the support of British was the most important factor for the growth of discontentment among the people.

These non-Manipuri traders, as the local people called 'Mayang' traders had started their industry inside a specific area in the heart of Imphal town, called 'British Reserve Area'. This area was completely under the administrative control of the British. Taking the advantage of this administrative position, the traders from outside started their business without any problem. Thus a large-scale influx of non-Manipuri traders had started to enter into Manipur just after the introduction of British colonial rule. However, in the general interest of the local people, the British treated them as foreigners and some restriction were put on them. Under the restriction the foreigners were permitted to stay for not more than the specified number of days allotted to them. Normally they were allowed to stay for not more than one week. If they wanted to stay further, they had to take permission from the concerned authority and had to pay Rupees five per year to the government. It was known as 'Foreigners' Tax'. This type of policy had undoubtedly played a major role in the process of the checking of a large-scale influx of foreigners into Manipur. In addition to this the British administrators also introduced another system, which was known as "Inner Line Permit System". Under this system every foreigner had to seek permission from the government while coming into the state. In order to deal with the matter of the foreigners the government also established a separate office known as 'Foreigner Department'. Besides foreigner's matter, this office also dealt with other five aspects. 1. Foreigners tax and grazing fees, 2. Income tax and trading license fees, 3. Cattle export, 4. Sales tax on cigarette or biri, and 5. Cart tax. Cart tax was abolished in August 1947.[19] The introduction of 'Foreigner Tax' and 'Inner Line Permit System' was a great boon for the people of Manipur because it rendered a very good protection to the local people from all the possible aspects of economic exploitation from the foreigners. This system was continued till Manipur was integrated into the Indian Union on 15th October, 1949. Then just after the merger the Socialist Party of both Manipur and Assam strongly urged the Indian Government to abolish it. According to them after the merger the people from outside Manipur cannot be treated as foreigners. The demand of the Socialist Party was strongly supported by the Congress party of Manipur.[20] Indeed, such type of development brought a new chapter in the economic and social life of the state. That it marked the beginning of the new social group in Manipur and on the other hand, it also paved a way for the beginning of a downward trend in the traditional economic system of the indigenous people. By endorsing the view of the Socialist Party, Himmat Singh, the Chief Commissioner of Manipur categorically said on the 9th of October, 1950 that all the people of both plains and hills areas should not be treated themselves as the people of this small state only. They should first try to treat themselves as the people of India.[21] On the basis of the demand of the socialist party and with the approval of the Indian Government, Himmat Singh abolished the system of restriction given to the people coming from outside on the 18th of November, 1950.[22] The abolition of this system was to open a flood gate for the influx of the trading class from outside Manipur and this caused a serious economic imbalance in this small state.

Just after the removal of the restriction, the traders from outside began to pour into Manipur and started to play a dominating role in the economy which was enjoyed by the indigenous people from time immemorial. First, they began to involve in the rice trading industry which is the only source of income of the local people. The Manipuris, because of their historical character and social environment, did not have even a basic knowledge of the art of export and import from the very early historical period. So, their vision and outlook in trade was very limited. This was basic weakness on the part of the local people and on the other hand this weakness was the strongest point of outside traders who were always looking for an opportunity. Taking the advantage of this situation they began to adopt the same policy which was practiced in India by the British before the outbreak of the industrial revolution. At that time, the British merchants, with the protection of the government had collected and procured all the articles and products at a fixed rate and they again sold it in the market at a high rate. This is just an example of that period. In Manipur also as a first step of wealth drain policy, the traders from outside concentrated their energy in the controlling of the export and import of rice. It is recorded that "owing to the lack of economic staying power of the people and their general backwardness, a few merchants who had established themselves in trade use to buy paddy immediately after harvest at the comparatively cheap prices and export outside the state and even sell them locally to new producers after a few months at exorbitant prices".[23] This fact was a clear indication of the degree of economic exploitation of the indigenous people of Manipur and this was the immediate result of the work of the post merger administrative establishment. In a memorandum submitted to the President of the Republic of India, the members of the "Assembly Demand Co-coordinating Committee" have categorically conveyed the disgusted feeling of the common people to the domination in the administration by the outsiders. They even said that this new process of the Indian Government in the administration was a system of "gradual de-Manipurization"[24]. They further said, "they are haughty, corrupt and ignorant of local conditions and very often mismanage and spoil things. They are not responsible to any one in Manipur and nor do they care the feeling, aspiration and interest of the Manipuri people."[25] Their monopoly in the export and import industry, that too with the help of the irresponsible bureaucrats had quickened the process of the exploitation of the traditional economic system of the local people. It is observed that if the people in the decision making bodies like legislative institution and executive level were sincere enough, such type of undesirable developments would not have occurred inspire of their (traders) best possible efforts to operate very effectively. Due to these conditions the genuine cultivators were not able to get a reasonable portion of the value of their work, which was due to the growth of such type of policy, and this was the legitimate cause for the growth of discontentment among the local agriculturist.[26]. With regard to the economic position of the state which was developed after the integration, it is observed that "the degree of the torture of the Himmat Singh's government had caused a serious imbalance in the minds of the people. In collusion with the capitalist section, they sucked the blood of the common people. They have looted the food of the people and on the other hand the Marwari traders have collected a large amount of money by using the illegal means. They have sent the spirit to the cotton yarn which was the soul of the Manipur womenfolk and because of this the traditional cottage industry of the indigenous people were also coming to the stage of extinction.[27]

It appears that there was no official restriction in the export of rice by the Marwari traders for a pretty long time. It is recorded that "to remedy this state of affairs and to reduce the disparity of the rice before and after harvest, the State Government with the approval of Indian

Government imposed a ban on the export of rice."[28] From these evidences it is quite clear that the government put restriction only after seeing the condition of the peasants. However, the export of rice was continued further. It is mentioned that certain amount of 'chira (flattened rice) was used for export to Assam. But the traders exported other local paddy of good quality in the guise of chira. To stop this, the government prohibited the export of chira.[29] The traders however gave a representation to the government for extending the export facility. But their request was not accepted on the ground of the bleak prospect of the current harvest. From these facts it can be suggested that the ban imposed by the State Government on the export of paddy and rice from Manipur was purely for a limited period of time. In an official report it is mentioned that the Manipur State imported 3,98,659 mounds, 27 seers, 13 chhattaks of rice from the central storage depots at Hojai, Gauhati and Calcutta.[30] In support of their policy it is also further mentioned that the import of rice was to meet the requirement of food grains. From this official note it can be observed why the government imported food grain from outside if there was enough procurement of rice or paddy. So, it may be suggested that perhaps the real motive of the government was to give maximum benefit to the outside traders by giving the facilities to export the good quality rice of Manipur to outside. In a memorandum submitted to the President of India the members of the Assembly Demand Co-coordinating Committee criticized the food policy of the government as not only callous and pro-hoarder, but also detrimental to the interest of the people.[31] They also said that the government left the entire administration of the market into the hands of hoarders, millers and traders.[32] The extension of all possible help to the outsiders in the matter of rice by the government was not a happy atmosphere to the people. However, they were not able to do anything as the people in the decision making body were all non-Manipuris. Such trend was treated by the revolutionary elements as a serious economic exploitation engineered by the agents of the Indian government.

In addition to this the government was not prepared to provide the scope for the promotion of the self-generating economic condition. There was no industry and no factory which could provide the job facility to the educated youth. This was also another important aspect which was strongly emphasized by the members of the revolutionary parties when they tried to justify their action. They were of the view that in this modern era industrialization was absolutely necessary for the improvement of the standard of living of the people. But the central leaders of India did not provide this facility to Manipur. They said that Manipur had a long history with a distinctive identity because of her rich economic facilities. But now after integration everything was changed and the new rulers gave little attention to the resource mobilization. As a result in the process of economic development Manipur was made a paralyzed state. They regarded such type of policy as a typical character of colonialism. They even criticized the Central leaders for adopting a policy to imbibe Manipuri in the habit of parasite culture. When enquired about the reason for discouraging the establishment of industries, the political leaders and policy makers were of the view that since Manipur is a border state it would not be feasible to establish industries. This type of negative attitude of the government was regarded by the younger generation as a challenge to their existence. They always resented the step-motherly treatment of the Indian leaders to the industrialization process in Manipur. One of the ex-revolutionary leaders argued that if Manipur was not allowed to extend the programme of industrialization why did they extend maximum industrial facility to other border states like Punjab, Rajasthan, Gujarat, West Bengal, etc. From this fact they came to the conclusion that the real intention of the government of India was to expand her territory but not in favour of the welfare of the people of Manipur. While giving their justification of their decision, they had pointed out the feeling of the people of Manipur at the time of integration. It is a fact that when the merger process was going on the feeling of the common people including the educated people was that merger of Manipur into India would bring prosperity and welfare of the people of this state. The people had a full confidence in the integrity of the Indian Government. They thought that since the leaders of the Indian Government had greatly been influenced by the democratic principles they would also extend an equal outlook to the people of Manipur. However that idea was not flourished just after the merger. Everything was changed beyond their expectation. Rather the bureaucrats even made an attempt to squeeze the system of traditional cottage industry. This fact was disclosed to the President of India in the form of a memorandum submitted by the members of the

'Assembly Demand Coordinating Committee'. They pointed out that the officers paid little interest to the development of industry. On the other hand a large quantity of industrial products of big industrial area began to pour into Manipur. Thus the coming of industrial products from outside Manipur finally led to the destruction of the whole economy of the state. To see this condition the educated youths began to observe Manipur as a victim of the internal colonialism. They began to say that Manipur's economy was at the mercy of the capitalist economic system of mainland India. This was just a market place for the industrial goods and agricultural products of the capitalist section of the mainland India. The revolutionary leaders thought that this situation was systematically created by the Indian Government in order to develop a habit of consumerism among the Manipuris. Instead of making Manipur a self-sufficient state she has become dependent heavily on Central Government. And gradually Manipur was forced to become a beggar state. They were of the view that such type of systematic economic exploitation would lead to the extinction of the real identity of Manipur. Even some section of the youths of Manipur who actively involved in the non-violent movement for the attainment of responsible government in the State, had strongly asserted that the policy of the Indian Government was a great insult to the prestige and identity of the national life of Manipuris. They warned the Central leaders with strong word that if no satisfactory change was made they would not be in a position to tolerate it and they would prepare to meet with determination any type of eventuality to protect the national prestige of Manipur. Having seen the experience of these negative economic development the educated youths began to observe that if Manipur continued to be a part of Indian Union, it would not be possible for the people of the state to save their identity. They also said the systematic undisclosed economic exploitation was a very serious issue on the question of the identity of the people. And so they advocated for a self-realization movement for the preservation of the economic identity of the people of Manipur. It is also observed that the deliberate refusal by the new administrators to transform the traditional economic system of Manipur in the tune of the modern economic development was a serious attempt to stop all the ways of economic life of the people of the state. In this respect some extremist elements was of the view that the main feature of this economic system was to keep Manipur as a captive market of India.[33] They further said that under this system Manipur became a ready market for the commodities of the industrial products of capitalist section of mainland India who had enjoyed the support of political leaders of Central Government. So in order to keep this market intact, no policy was adopted for getting opportunity of self-generating economic condition. Therefore, the new trend of economic conditions which was developed just after the merger into India has created a good reason for the growth of separatist tendencies among the people particularly the younger generation of Manipur.

## DOMINATION OF OUTSIDERS IN THE ADMINISTRATION

The feeling of unhappiness among the local people towards the new political and economic set up which developed after the merger was further intensified by the degree of the domination of outsiders in the state administration. It is opined that under this systematic political subjugation, the major departments of the government were headed by persons who came from the other parts of India and so the Manipuris were not given due importance in the administration.[34] The impact of this domination by outsiders had greatly helped the growth of the idea of self-determination among the educated young people of Manipur. It is a fact that just after integration Manipur was put in the category of the Part C State under the Indian Constitution and the State was kept under the direct administration of the Centre. In order to make more convenient to them the Center appointed the non-Manipuri officials in all the key positions in the administration. In the Secretariat, Revenue Department, Education, Medicine, etc. all the heads of departments were non-Manipuris in spite of the fact that there were qualified local people for these positions. This sudden change was regarded by the younger generation as a kind of insult and encroachment to the right and privilege of the local people. On the other hand, those non-Manipuri officers did not care about the feelings, aspiration and interest of the local people. In a memorandum submitted to the President of India on the 3rd of April, 1960, the Assembly Demand Coordinating Committee pointed out the negative attitude of the non-Manipuri officers towards the local people, with whom they had to deal with. They also criticized the non-Manipuri officers for their deliberate ignorance of the Manipuri language which is the official language of the state. During the colonial period in spire of many undesirable administrative policy. the British officers always tried to mix up with the people by learning the language of the local people. Within six months such type of policy had quickly enhanced the degree of understanding between the common people and colonial officers. In addition to this they also claimed that most of these officers who were sent to Manipur had created an ill feeling among the local people. The reason for the development of such type of undesirable feeling was created by these officers. They did not care the feelings, aspiration and interest of the Manipuri people. In fact, they were not responsible to any one in Manipur because they thought that the power of suppression, dismissal and transfer was with the Central Government not with the local government. Therefore their only interest was to keep a good relationship with the Central Government so that their interest could be well protected. They did not pay much attention to the welfare of the people and development of the state. Due to this deliberate ignorance in all the developmental aspects the condition of the people was declining at a great pace despite their lip service to the people. The number of educated unemployed youths had increased and they began to face a serious handicap in their search for jobs as many of these posts were held by the people of outside Manipur. The revolutionary youths called them "imported people" from outside.

Since there were no scope for employment opportunity a large number of educated young people had become frustrated with the administration dominated by the outsiders. The degree of the persistent rise of irresistible feelings of discontent and frustration particularly among them was mainly due to the long unsuited autocratic rule of the Chief Commissioner, because under this bureaucratic administrative set-up the local people had no chance to enter into the responsible position of the government. Actually, there were a lot of local people who would be able to run the department smoothly and efficiently. But the non-Manipuri bureaucrats did not take them into confidence at the crucial stage of any public decision. These officers were directly appointed by the Ministry of Home Affairs in consultation with Chief Commissioner. In a memorandum submitted to the President of India the Manipur Youth Assembly Demand Committee had criticized the attitude of the non-Manipuri officers and alleged that they gave a free hand to the non-Manipuri smugglers. Thus, they made fortune by illegal means.[35] In fact, under the system of the non-Manipuri bureaucratic set-up of administration, the final decision was in the hands of these outsiders and not with the local people. Therefore this exploitation of the people and all their available resources by the non-Manipuri officers appointed by the Centre in the name of national integrity became a never blotted cause of inducing anti-national feelings among the Manipuris.[36] In an open letter to the Ministers of the Indian Government, L. Achou Singh, the Member of Parliament, severely criticized the attitude of the non-Manipuri bureaucrats particularly their policy of discrimination in the appointment of people in the important positions under the Manipur administration. He pointed out that the non-Manipuri officers had imported "their own kith and kin" to appoint in the respective administrative position of the State Government. In regard to their effectiveness it was observed that these officers might have been sent by the Central Government because either they were inefficient or incompetent or unwanted. To see this condition all the members of the political parties and youths expressed their unhappiness for making Manipur as the asylum centre for all the inefficient non-Manipuri officers. So domination by non-Manipuri officers in the administration of the state was regarded by the people of the younger generation as a kind of the policy of the internal colonialism of the Central Government of India. They strongly felt that this policy would bring a serious negative impact to the identity of the self-governing character of the people of Manipur. In addition to this the degree of corruption in the administration of the state was also another very disappointing aspect of the people of this state particularly the youths. They were of the view that the growth of the degree of corruption was the work of these non-Manipuri officers. Therefore domination had crated a negative attitude and mistrust in the minds of local people towards the non-Manipuri people in general and the leadership of the Government of India in particular.

## CULTURE

The socio-religious changes which had taken place in Manipur from the time of the advent of Hindu religion vis-à-vis the Sanskritisation process which was enforced in the social life of the people was also another important contributing factor for the growth of separatist tendency among the people of Manipur. Though it is not required to go into detail about the process of the coming of Hinduism in Manipur, it is quite evident that there were a sharp radical change in the social life of the state just after the introduction of Hindu religion from the first quarter of the 18th century. The successful attempt of Shanti Das, a Hindu preacher to intensify the philosophy and religious practices of Hinduism, had produced a far-reaching impact in the social life of the common people. His effort was so powerful that during one generation, the social, cultural and even the racial identity of the people of Manipur particularly the Meitei people in the valley areas was radically Sankritised.[37] The biggest negative impact of the Sanskritisation process on the local people was the stratification of the society. It is a well-known fact that the society of Manipur before the coming of Hinduism was a casteless society. So, there was no question on the issue of the inequality among the people. Then with the conversion to Hinduism all the Meitei people including the king were declared as Kshetriyas. Among the Kshetriyas, the people of the ruling elite group was known as 'Rajkumar'. A separate group outside the Meitei was again formed known as 'Brahmin group'. In addition to this so many unprecedented taboos were also introduced under the new religious practices which forced the people to accept it. The burning of 'Puyas', the sacred literary works of the people, at the instigation of Shanti Das was a remarkable example of the cultural imperialism of the Hindu religion. Destruction of the abodes of traditional deities and fanatic action of destruction of the images of 'Umanglais'[38] and construction of temple for the Hindu deities was also another special feature of the Hindu colonialism process. All these works of fanatics were successfully performed with the help of the king.

From the evidences, the basic objectives and intention of Shanti Das was to transform the whole society of Manipur into Hindu society and Hindu way of life. He also wanted to give a very good reflection of this new conceptual outlook even to the political system of the state. One of the most successful theory propagated under the system of Sanskritisation is the theory of the 'Mahabharat's Manipur' and introduction of one Babhruvahan as the ruler of Manipur. The theory of the father and son relationship between the hero of Mahabharata, Arjuna and Babhruvahan was so deep rooted that even today many believed that 'Rajkumar' families of Manipur are the descendents of 'Surya Vansa' or Solar Dynasty to which Arjuna belonged. Apart from this the title 'Maharaja' was given to the king and the present name of the state, Manipur was also coined after the introduction of Hindu religion.

The adoption of Hindu names for all the rivers, hills, lakes, months, etc. was also another important interesting feature of 'Sanskritisation' process. Even the original names of the ancient kings were changed into Hindu names. The traditional name "Salai' or clan of the Meiteis was changed as 'Gotra'. The different traditional names of the clans were changed to Hindu names. The Ningthouja, the traditional clan name of the king's dynasty is changed to Hindu name 'Shandilya Gotra'. Likewise 'Angom' was changed as 'Kaushika', the Chenglei (Sarang Leishangthem) as Bhardwaj, the Luwang as Kahyap, the Khuman as Madhugalya, the Mangang as Aitereya and Khaba Nganba as Goutam. The traditional name of 'Nongda Lairen Pakhangba' who was regarded as the first historical king of Manipur and the founder of 'Ningthouja' dynasty was changed as 'Yabistha' and the other kings were also given Hindu names. They gave new Hindu names to all the hills, rivers and lakes in this state. For example, some important hills which are regarded as sacred traditional religious places of the people like (i) The Koubru Ching, (ii) Heibok Ching, (iii) Nongmaijing Hills, etc. were named as 'Koumer Parbat', 'Bhagleshore Giri', 'Nilakantha Giri', etc., according to the Hindu religion. The Imphal river was changed to 'Vijya Nadi', the Iril River as 'Iranadi', the Kongba River as 'Gaibi Ganga', etc. The 'Nungjeng Pukhri', a very important sacred religious tank inside the Kangla was named as 'Bindu Sorobor, and Loktak Lake as 'Lakshi Bhil', 'Pumlenpat' another lake as 'Poulemba', Moirang as 'Mahirangapur' and Lamphelpat as 'Sangai Yumpham', etc.[39] Apart from this all the important traditional festivals of the people of this area were successfully identified with the Hindu festivals. For example the 'Waira Tenkap Festival' (Archery), an important sports festivals organized annually in the month of Fairel (January/February) was converted into a 'Kirtan of Lord Rama', the 'Poirei Apakna' of the month of Lamda (March) was converted to 'Loipam' festival, the 'Kongba Leithong Phatpa' ceremony which was held in the month of Sajibu (April) was equated by 'Ratha Jatra', the offering to the ancestors in the month of September was substituted by 'Tarpan' (offering to Pritulok), the 'Wakambung Chingnung Nongoibi' performed in the month of Mera (October) was substituted by 'The Sana Kwaktanba of Durga Puja or Dushera', the 'Chanouhui Chinten' (New harvest) by 'Govardhan Puja', the annual boat festival of 'Ayang Yoiren Iruppa' in the month of Wakching (December/January) was also changed as an annual 'Snan' (ritual bathing) at Lilong Sahonpat.[40]

The Sanskritisation process started from the time of king Garibaniwaz was further consolidated during the time of Bheigyachandra. During his time Vaishnava cult flourished in Manipur. Another significant feature of this period was the increase of the influence of the Bengali cultural influence. It is rightly said that "Since the religious preachers were Bengali speakers preaching Bengali school of Vaishnavism, the Hinduisation of Manipur was influenced by the Bengali language and literature"[41]. Their influence was very strong and it came in the form of change into dress, food habit and Bengali language as the medium of religious transactions, either in signing of hymns or writings. Along with this, influence of the Brahmins became very strong and their presence and participation became an inevitable part of the life of the common people. Gradually, the domination of the Brahmins in the social life of the people had increased and the common people began to forget the concepts and practices of the traditional religion. Taking the advantages of the existing social condition the Brahmin group introduced so many norms and practices and ultimately it led to the divisions among the different groups of people in Manipur. The influence of Hinduism and dominating role of the Brahmin group was so strong that even the Christian Missionary People failed in their attempt to start their missionary activities in the valley area. Then they moved to the hill areas of Manipur and successfully started their missionary activities. Ultimately it laid the foundation for the dichotomy between the hill people and plain people in their ideology and practices. Such type of undesirable social and culture relationship which was developed between the hill people and plain people was the deliberate contribution of the cultural imperialistic policy of the Brahmin group.

The importance and influence of this group was tremendously increased from the middle of the 19th century. The Hindu religious practices became the social order of the society and the position of the Brahmin group also reached its zenith. A sharp difference was created between the Brahmin and the common people. In addition to this a policy of ostracism was adopted and under this policy so many social evils like 'Mangba and Shengba' (clean and unclean), were introduced. Taking the advantage of this system the Brahmin group with the full support of feudal rulers outcasted a large number of people including their family on many flimsy grounds. As a result of this many people became the victim of this evil policy. Apart from this, in order to make their position more secure in the society a myth was created and according to this myth if the Brahmin holds the plough in the paddy field it was a great omen for the country. So under this belief the Brahmins were free from doing any type of cultivable work. Thus they lived very happily with the help of other groups of people.

The authoritarian and dominating role of the Brahmin group and their endless effort to make Manipur as a Hinduised society had produced an in equilibrium among different strata of the society. Gradually the people, with a great care, began to express their 'Anti-Brahmin' felling in a very low tone. The superiority feeling and attitude of the 'Brahmin group' had created unhappiness particularly among the younger generation. They began to feel that such type of the policy of cultural imperialism under the Sanskritisation process would definitely effect their traditional cultural identity and it would lead to the final extinction of the identity of the people who belong to the Mongoloid group. So, gradually the idea of the protection and preservation of the cultural identity and traditional social practices of the Manipuri people began to develop in the minds of the radical group of people. The first reaction was initiated by Naoria Phullo, who was widely regarded among the revivalist group as 'Laininghal', in the year 1930 by establishing a social and religious organisation known as 'Apokpa Marup' at Cachar. Under this organisation he made a successful attempt to revive the ideas and practices of the traditional religious believe of the Manipuri people and the history of this place. From Cachar the activities and the ideas of Naoria Phullo came to Manipur and many young people began to associate with his philosophy for the protection of the identity of the people of this state. Thus, from the anti-Brahmin stand the dimension of the movement extended to a large perspective of the preservation of the national cultural identity of the people of this state. However the intensity of the movement was not very strong before integration of Manipur into

India. At that time more than ninety percent of the total population particularly of the valley area had been greatly influenced by the practice and concept of Hindu religion. Therefore, their mind and outlook were always towards the West i.e., India. Even educated people of that time firmly believed that Manipur would be more prosperous if she was integrated into India. This idea was reflected in the resolution of the Manipur State Congress Party which was established at the initiative of the educated people of that period. The resolution strongly asserted that if Manipur were integrated into India, she would be definitely a welfare state. The coming of this idea was mainly due to the influence of cultural imperialism of Hindu religion.

The post-merger political and economic development in Manipur was the most important and remarkable contributing factor for the strengthening of the idea of the preservation of the national identity of the Manipuri people. The nature of the political and economic development in Manipur and attitude of the leaders of the Central Government just after the merger into India produced a negative feeling. Seeing the negative developmental process the people, particularly the young educated people, began to feel that the only answer to the motive and attitude of the Indian leaders was to maintain and preserve the distinctive identity of the Manipuri people. They also felt that the psychological state of the people of Manipur was mainly due to the influence of the Hindu religion and Sanskritisation process. So, to remove this influence, they began to revive the past glory and pride and the traditional religious concept and practices of the people of this state. A large section of the youths began to participate in the revivalist movement which was launched by the 'Apokpa Marup' under the leadership of Naoria Phullo.

The establishment of 'Apokpa Marup' as a social and religious organisation with the basic objective to protect and maintain the historical identity of the Manipuri people was indeed a remarkable development in the history of Manipur. It awakened the mind and the spirit of the people for the establishment of a new social and religious order on the foundation of their traditional religious beliefs and custom. The question of the existence and identity of the people of this area was also an indirect outcome of the movement of this organisation. N. Bisheswar, the founder leader of PLA (Eastern Region) said that the adoption of Hinduism was the only reason for the extinction of the separate and distinctive cultural identity of the people of Manipur.[42] Professor Gangmumei also observed that the genesis of the identity crisis can be traced to the Sanskritisation of Manipur.[43] After having a thorough and systematic thinking, the people now fully realized that ethnically, the people of Manipur belonged to the Mongoloid group not Aryan. The people no longer believed the theory of the Mahabharata's Manipur as well as the theory of the Aryan origin. They also began to condemn the cultural imperialistic policy of the Hinduism and efforts of the Brahmin' group. Thus, a serious problem of identity crisis was developed in the minds of the people after merger of Manipur into India. A large number of young people began to take initiative for the establishment of a separate identity based on the traditional religious concept and custom. In order to materialize the objective they began to make a serious campaign among the common people to remember the history and traditional culture of this state. In an open letter addressed to the people of Manipur they wrote, "some of our kings have brought many greedy Brahmins who bought with them their orthodox and false notion of god and goddesses. They have deceived our scientific religion and burned down our library. Caste system was introduced to us and thus the division between us started".[44] It further mentioned that their culture, both in the hills and plains had been forced to degenerate to the level of the aboriginal and, Indian culture was being forced on them. Their nationalism was gradually converted to tribalism. With this observation they were of the view that due to the loss of the genetically ablest stains of their population, they have to face the present crisis. So, they said that it was by their sons and daughters who help the Indians to occupy their motherland. They had to ask them to return their land or leave this land[45]. An ex-revolutionary leader said that the flames of the insurgency broke out mainly because of the anger of the youths at the losing of their traditional ethnic cultural identity created by the conversion of Vaishnava Hinduism as state religion with the support of the rulers.[46] Thus, anti-Hinduism stand adopted by the revivalist section among the people of Manipur had also rendered a significant help to the growth of the separatist tendency in this state. Their strong campaign for the protection and preservation of the traditional cultural outlook gave a strong impetus for the preservation of the national identity of the Manipuri people.

Lt. General V.K. Nayar, who was the Governor of Manipur, had categorically stated that the feeling of discontent, sub-nationalism and concept of secessionism are the outcome of the policy of alienation even when they were part of the national reinsure. Therefore, the cultural revivation and ethnic resurgent was the natural outcome pre-situation.[47]

## NOTES

1. Kabui, Gangmumei. 'Insurgency in Manipur Valley'. A seminar paper presented on The North East Regional Problems and Perspective, Chandigarh, April 27 to May 1, 1981.
2. Ibid.
3. Shyamkanhai, Ksh. 'Merger of Manipur with India'. Seminar paper presented at 3rd Session of HEIHA, Imphal 6-8 Dec. 1982.
4. Majumdar, R.C., H.C. Roychoudhury and A.K. Dutta.1965. *An Advance History of India*, P. 998.
5. Letter from Shri Prakash to Maharaja of Manipur. 4.7.49.
6. Secret Memorandum No. 2601 P.1-1 dated 25.6.49.
7. Letter dated 19.9.49 from Shri Prakash, the Governor of Assam to Maharaja of Manipur
8. *Jawaharlal Nehru's Speech*. Vol.1. Published by Publication Division, Ministry of Information and Broadcasting. P.72.
9. Majumdar, R.C., H.C. Roychoudhury and A.K. Dutta. Op.cit. Pp 999-1000.
10. Kabui, Gangmumei. Op.cit. (Seminar paper)
11. *Prajatantra* (A local Manipur Daily). 13.4.53.
12. *Committees and Commisions in India*. 1947-73. Vol.1.
13. *Prajatantra*. 25.4.53.
14. Memorandum submitted to the State Reorganization Commission. April, 1954.
15. Ibid.
16. Seminar on 'Insurgency in Manipur: Search for an Answer'. Organized by Committee of Concerned Citizen at Imphal.
17. Dena, Lal. 'Roots of Separatist movement in North East India'' (Seminar paper).
18. Nkrunhe, Kwane. 1973. *Neo-Colonialism, The Last Stage of Imperialism*. P.IX.
19. *Annual Administrative Report of Manipur*. 1946-47. P.16.

20. Shyamkanhai. Ksh. Op.cit. P.10.
21. *The Gazetteer of Manipur*. 1950. Op.cit. P.10.
22. Shyamkanhai. Ksh. Op.cit. P.10.
23. *Annual Administrative Report of Manipur*. 1954. P.2.
24. *Why Responsible Government of Manipur*. P.17.
25. Ibid.
26. Ibid.
27. Shyamkanhai. Ksh. Op.cit. P.22.
28. *Annual Administrative Report of Manipur*. 1954. P.2.
29. *Annual Administrative Report of Manipur*. 1975. P.13.
30. *Manipur Territory Annual Administrative Report for 1960-61*. P.87.
31. Memorandum submitted to the President of India on 3rd April. 1960 by Assembly Dem and Co-Coordinating Committee.
32. Ibid.
33. 'Oppose Indian Annexation Month September 21 to October 15. 1994'. Published by United National Liberation Front.
34. *Youths' Mental Unrest in Manipur*. Published by National Research Centre (NRC). P.9.
35. Memorandum submitted by the Manipur Youth Assembly Demand Committee to the President of India for the restoration of responsible government in Manipur
36. Ibid.
37. Kamei, Gangmumei. 1991. *History of Manipur, Pre-Colonial Period*. P. 257.
38. It is the presiding deities of village, clan and lineage.
39. Jhulon, M. *Vijay Panchalli*. P.2.
40. *Sanamahi Laikan*. Pp.59-60.
41. Kamei, Gangmumei. Op.cit. P.72.
42. Bisheshwor, N. 1986. *The Last Expression on My Death Bed*. P.15
43. Commemorative Volume of *'Freedom'*. Daily English newspaper. Dec.12. 1994.
44. Political Thesis of Manipur. P.5. (An open letter to the people of Manipur).
45. Ibid
46. Labango, P. 1997. *Kangleipak Revolution*. P.1
47. Nayar, V.K. Lt. General (Retd.).2000. *Law Intensity Conflict of India*. Pp. 67-98.

CHAPTER THREE

# NATURE AND CHARACTER OF THE REVOLUTIONARY ORGANISATIONS

## THE MEITEI STATE COMMITTEE (M.S.C.)

In an official statement, the Government of Manipur, after giving some critical observations about the law and order situation, observed that although the situation was quite normal "but, for some Meitei criminals, who in collaboration with Naga underground, constituted themselves into the so-called Meitei State Committee for sabotage, including unsuccessful instigation of Manipuri youth to bear arms against the Government like their Naga and Mizo counterparts, for the avowed aim of the Committee to set up an autonomous Meitei state in their independent Nagaland".[1] R. Constantine projected the leaders and other members of this organisation as a "disoriented left wing elements".[2] He further said that "mere desperados did not produce much affect on the political scene".[3] It is also observed that although the Meitei State Committee was established by 20/30 uneducated persons it became the centre of attraction to the educated youths of Manipur.[4] These were the views and observations of the different platforms and writers. But the Meitei State Committee as an armed underground with a sole objective to establish a separate independent state of Manipur was, indeed, an eye opener to the ongoing process of the normal political and social life of the country. As has been mentioned above, the emergence of the idea of separatism was a spontaneous outburst of the effect of accumulated grievances disillusioned by the people from the time of the integration of this state into India.

An official record mentioned that the Meitei State Committee was a militant organisation which was formed under the initiative of some ex-members of the Communist Party. However, in a press release issued by Kangleipak Communist Party (KCP), it is mentioned that Meitei State Committee was formed by seven members on 7th January, 1967 at the hill of Thangal Surung[5] and officially it came into existence on 12th January, 1967. This press note was issued after having a meeting of the Committee on 15th July, 1994. This organisation was established under a full understanding with the leaders of Naga Underground Movement. It is also recorded that "The Meitei State Committee was affiliated to the so-called Federal Government of Nagaland on 14. 1. 67." Further it is also mentioned that the idea for the establishment of an armed organisation against the Government of India emerged for the first time in the last quarter of the year 1966 and it was established under a full understanding with the leaders of the Naga underground organisation. The idea for the formation of an underground organisation and the establishment of relationship with the leaders of the Naga underground was first initiated by some Meitei youths from Chandrakhong and Ukhongsang villages, who were at that time actively involved as members of the Naga underground movement. They were sent by the Naga underground leaders to meet the ex-revolutionaries of the armed movement of 1948. Their sole objective was to make a common front for the maintenance of the identity of the people of this region and to spread their activities throughout the entire areas of the North-Eastern Region. First, they came to Wangkheirakpam Tomba Singh who was a close associate of H. Irabot Singh during the period of the armed movement of 1948-51 and a leader of the Communist party. They informed him about the desire of the leaders of the Naga underground and they even requested him to go along with them. Tomba Singh thought that it was a good opportunity for them if they wished to follow the political line adopted by their late leader H. Irabot Singh. He said that the only desire of Irabot Singh was to bring a new social and political set-up through armed movement with the help and co-operation of the surrounding hill people. He believed that no successful revolution in Manipur could be launched without the co-operation and active participation of the hill people. But his untimely death brought a disastrous effect to his revolutionary process. Therefore according to Tomba Singh, the only way to translate the dream of their late leader into action was to set up a revolutionary party and follow the political concept and path of H. Irabot Singh. On the basic foundation of this belief he discussed this matter with other ex-revolutionaries. They also agreed the proposal of the Naga Underground.

In the meantime, the leaders of the Naga Underground again requested him to extend his support to their cause.[6] With the full understanding of his colleagues Tomba Singh prepared to meet the Naga underground leaders. First he went to Thangal village. He stayed there for a single night. In the morning of the next day he was escorted to Kangpokpi by some underground people and from there he went to Nagaland and met the leaders at a place called 'Tidima'.[7] The talk between Tomba Singh and the Naga leaders was held through an interpreter. His name was Nileh[8], a youth of Mao Naga tribe of Manipur. In their talk the Naga leaders expressed their desire to know the history of the relationship between Naga and Meitei people and they also wanted to consolidate the solidarity which was enjoyed both by Naga people and Meitei people from the early historical period. They also requested him to contact Sagolsem Indramani Singh of Thangmeiband as he had already visited Nagaland with a view to establish contact with the leaders of the Naga underground.[9] The Naga leaders categorically stated that their only desire was to launch an armed movement in Manipur so that they would be able to maintain a separate political identity outside India. Just after returning from Nagaland, Tomba went to the house of some Meitei scholars to get the history of the relationship between Naga and Meitei people. He got it from one Mohori Singh Yairipok and it was translated into English and sent to Naga leaders. Then Naga leaders also agreed to extend full co-operation and asked him to organise for an armed movement.

After getting all the possible assurances about the possible all sorts of help and to materialise the political line of Hijam Irabot, Tomba Singh formed a preparatory committee of twenty-five members.[10] They were:

| Sl. No. | Name | Address |
|---|---|---|
| 1. | Manglem Singh | Awangjiri |
| 2. | Laphoi Singh | Kamabong |
| 3. | Heikrujam Meino Singh | Heikrujam |
| 4. | Puyam Mohori Singh | Yairipok |
| 5. | A friend of Mohori Singh | Yairipok |
| 6. | Hijam Makar Singh | Mantripukhri |
| 7. | Oinam Kalachand Singh | Laipham Khunou |
| 8. | Angom Yaima Singh | Kanglatongbi |
| 9. | Laishram Yaima Singh | Kanglatongbi |
| 10. | Elangbam Mangi Singh Thongam Leikai | Singjamei |
| 11. | Kshetrimayum Achoubi Singh Kshetri Leikai | Singjamei |
| 12. | Kshetrimayum Moirangningthou | Mayang Imphal |
| 13. | Lai Tomal Singh | Kumbi |
| 14. | Thambal Singh | Chairen |
| 15. | Selung Singh | Naharup |
| 16. | Waikhom Kulla Singh | Khurai |
| 17. | Sarangthem Mani Singh | Wakhong |
| 18. | Pukhrambam Tomba Singh | Wakhong |
| 19. | Angom Ibohal Singh | Patlou |
| 20. | Ngangkham Babu Singh | Laitonpokpi |
| 21. | Salam Sanatomba Singh | Laitonpokpi |
| 22. | Brahmacharimayum Samungouba Sharma | Keibi |
| 23. | Ningthoukhongjam Mani Singh | Keibi |
| 24. | Wangkheirakpam Tomba Singh | Keibi |
| 25. | Rajkumar Kullasana Singh Khunou | Laipham |

The first meeting of this preparatory committee was held in the month of October 1966 at the residence of Phukhrambam Tomba Singh of Wakhong village. In that meeting all of them agreed to establish an armed underground revolutionary organisation under the name of 'Manipur State Committee'. But it is said that this proposed name was not acceptable to the Naga leaders. They were of the view that since they fought for the Nagas, the question of covering the whole Manipur was not advisable. So, they insisted to form an organisation only for the valley area.[11] The members were not able to bring a consensus opinion about the starting point of their action. Some members expressed their desire to start the action from border areas of Mizoram. But some suggested that action should be started from the surrounding hill areas of Manipur. Accordingly another meeting was held at the residence of one Abung of Thangal Surung, a tribal village situated at a distance of about 30 miles from Imphal. It is said that some Naga underground leaders were also invited in that meeting. The discussion continued for three days from 11th to 13th January 1967[12]. The members who attended the meeting were:-

| Sl. No. | Name | Address |
|---|---|---|
| 1.. | W. Tomba Singh | Keibi |
| 2. | B. Shamungou Sharma | Keibi |
| 3. | N. Mani Singh | Keibi |
| 4. | Thambal Singh | Chairen |
| 5. | Lai Tomal | Kumbi |
| 6. | Ksh. Moirangningthou | Mayang Imphal |
| 7. | Ksh. Achoubi Leikai | Singjamei Kshtri |
| 8. | E. Mangi Thongam Leikai | Singjamei |
| 9. | L. Yaima | Kanglatongbi |
| 10. | Angom Yaima | Ngairangbam |
| 11. | A. Ibohal | Patlou |
| 12. | S. Mani | Wakhong |
| 13. | N. Babu | Leitanpokpam |
| 14. | S. Sanatomba | Leitanpokpam |

In this meeting the proposed name of this organisation was changed from the 'Manipur State Committee' to the 'Meitei State Committee'. Thus after this meeting the 'Meitei State Committee' emerged as an armed revolutionary party in Manipur. According to an official record the existence of the Meitei State Committee came to the notice of the people with a circulation of a hand written cyclostyled leaflet under the caption 'Prajasingda Khanghanjaba' (notice to the people) at Lamlai, a village situated to the northern side of Imphal in May 1967 signed by K.S. Angami, Secretary to the President. It further said that this man was later on identified as one Apabi Sharma.

As has been mentioned above the basic aim and objective of the Meitei State Committee was to establish Manipur as an independent state. Another aim of the organisation was to join hands with other revolutionary groups of the other sister states of North-Eastern region of India for having a separate political identity of these areas and they wanted to fix the boundary line of the proposed state between Brahmaputra and Ningthee rivers.[13] In order to materialise their objective into action Shri Tomba Singh went to Nagaland and met some Naga leaders. After having some positive understanding the Naga leaders agreed to extend all sorts of necessary help to Meitei State Committee. As an initial step they gave some small firearms and ammunition. It is said that with the help of these arms the members of the Meitei State Committee were able to collect some money and arms. Then they again returned those small arms to the Naga leaders.

The organisational structure of the Meitei State Committee was based on two important wings, i.e., civil and military. The civil wing carried out the entire responsibilities of the general administration of the organisation including the fund collection, publicity works and recruitment, etc. The armed action was carried on under the care of military wing. But later on with an objective to make it more effective the management of military wing was put under a committee of three persons. They were: (1) Hourangbam Angou Singh of Lousangkhong village, (2) Rengdol, a Kom tribe of Utonglok village near Leitanpokpi, and (3) Soibam Yaima Singh of Patlou village. There were no specific recruitment rules of the Meitei State Committee but majority of the members of the armed wing of the organisation were from the ex-members of the then armed revolutionary movement of 1948. These group of people remained silent just after the death of their leader H. Irabot Singh. They all came out and joined the organisation of Meitei State Committee as they believed that the objective and policy of this armed movement was not different from the concept of Late H. Irabot Singh. After completion of full preparation they started to give military training. It is mentioned that earlier they planned to send only twelve persons but due to certain unavoidable circumstances the number of trainees was increased to seventeen.[14] Whereas according to an official document the president of the Meitei State Committee sent thirteen members to the underground Naga camp at Maram on 9th April 1967, to undergo training for the use of firearms and bombs. It is also further mentioned that some more members also received training from the Naga underground at Tora, Ukhrul.

At the beginning the revolutionary activities of the Meitei State Committee was confined mainly in the Keibi village and its surrounding areas. Then gradually their activities began to spread to the other areas and thus they were able even to attract the attention of the well-educated youths of the urban areas and some of them began to involve in the revolutionary activities of the Meitei State Committee. The activities of the volunteers of Meitei State Committee became a great concern to the state government. On the other hand their revolutionary activities had created a serious disturbance in the law and order situation of the state. While their revolutionary activities was in full swing the position of the Commander-in-Chief of the armed wing was changed from Ramchandra to one Shri Ito Singh of Salungpham village. An official record mentioned that "the volunteers of the Meitei State Committee were planning to destroy a bridge in the Sekmai-Khurkhul road by using bombs in 1968. But police got the information in time and the bomb was defused". Such type of activities brought a serious problem to the administration of the state. On top of this, their relation with the Federal Government of Nagaland had created a serious concern to the government particularly on the issue of national integrity. Keeping this view in their mind and in order to bring normalcy in the state, the government had adopted a repressive measure against the Meitei State Committee. After having some positive result in their activities, the volunteers of the Committee established a base camp near Purum Likli and from this area they began to operate in other surrounding areas. But unfortunately the information of their whereabouts reached the knowledge of the government very soon. Immediately a large police force was sent to that area and an exchange of fire took place between the volunteers of the Committee and police personnel at Purum Ching. In this encounter Ito Singh, the Commander-in-Chief was killed and a large numbeer of volunteers were arrested. According to an official record the police apprehended about 63 persons and arrested a large number of important persons of the Meitei State Committee. Then the police party raided the hideouts of the organisation and seized many arms and explosives. They were: (1) 23 detonators, (2) 6 detonators fused with wire, (3) metals, (4) 3 time switch, (5) 2 time switch (Nos. nil) with rubber cap, (6) 6 time switch No 10 MK, (7) 1 white fuse wire length about 38' 1", (8) 1 red fuse wire length about 19' 6", (9) 5 spare parts of time switch, (10) 1 spare part of time switch with rubber cap, (11) Gun powder weighing 2 k.g., (12) 1 (LMG) unserviceable, and (13) 1 bomb without cap.

The untimely death of Ito Singh produced a serious debacle to the organisational activities of the Meitei State Committee and at the same time it also gave a severe set back in the morals of the volunteers. After this incident the members of the organisation were not able to do much revolutionary activities. Indeed, after this incident the work of the organisation had seriously declined. This development was a great opportunity to the state government. Taking the opportunity of this deteriorating condition in the working of the revolutionary movement the government also tried to weaken their strength by adopting several type of policies. The main objective of the State government was to create a serious division among the rank and file of the organisation. So, in order to materialise this objective they declared that the state government was ready to provide the maximum facilities to those volunteers of the Manipur State Committee if they surrendered to the government. The plan of the government was so effective that after this declaration a large number of volunteers surrendered to the government. Among them the most important leader who surrendered to the government was Rangdol, who was an important member of the management of the armed wing of the organisation. The government immediately gave him Rupees two thousand under the rehabilitation programme. Such political decision taken by a prominent leader like him was, indeed, a serious set back to the moral and activities of the members of the organisation. After him many members of the organisation also had surrendered to the State government and all of them got Rupees two thousand each under the rehabilitation programme of the government. Some other members who received the money from the state government were: (1) Angom Ibohal Singh of Patlou, (2) Sarangthem Mani Singh of Wakhong. (3) Oinam Tombi Singh of Keibi Heikak. etc. Besides them there were some other members who received the same amount of money from the state government. In the meantime police also arrested a large number of members of the organisation and they were put in jail. At last Wangkheimayum Tomba Singh, the leader of the organisation, was arrested by the police from the house of Shri Mohori Singh of Yairipok village. He was put in jail till 1973. The government offered him money, but he did not accept it. It has rightly been observed that the Meitei State Committee did not present much of a challenge to the police. It withered easily and 'unheroically, under the pressure of law and order.[15] Thus his arrest brought the end of the revolutionary activities of the Meitei State Committee. It is recorded that the Meitei State committee had been virtually smashed in the year 1970-71[16] and finally became extinct in the year 1971-72. Hence the revolutionary activities of the Meitei State Committee was completely smashed when it was just at an infant stage.

Many factors were responsible for the failure of the activities of the Meitei State Committee. The lack of intellectual cohesiveness among the rank and file of the organisation was one of the causes for the failure of this organisation. It is a fact that all the important members of the organisation including the leader had little knowledge about the concept of the modern revolutionary movement. It was mainly because of their lack of knowledge and proper education. Due to this condition they were not able to give a proper theoretical guideline to the volunteers, which is the most important prerequisite factor for the success of any type of armed revolutionary movement. As a result of this lack of intellectual and theoretical background the leaders of the movement faced a serious problem at the time of organising the activities of the movement. In this respect it can be mentioned that the success and failure of any type of mass movement entirely depend on the participation either physically or morally of the people. It is a fact that no movement was able to go smoothly without the help of the people. Whereas in the case of the activities of the Meitei State Committee the degree of response to the movement was very low because the leaders of the movement were not able to give a clear picture about the aim and objective of the movement to the people. As it has already been mentioned above the movement started simply because they wanted to continue the political line adopted by Shri H. Irabot Singh. On the other side, the government, with the help of their propaganda work, was able to create a different picture about the activities of the movement. They were able to project the activities of the Meitei State Committee as anti-social. The propaganda of the government was so effective that the people particularly the urban elites were afraid of the members of this organisation. Such type of tendency was mainly due to the lack of intellectual depth among the rank and file of the organisation. In addition to this the lack of cohesiveness in the system of organisation was also another factor. It is a well-known fact that the movement was started when the functioning of the organisation was not yet properly maintained. The greatest tragedy on the part of the leaders was that they were not able to read the political mind of the people of Manipur. Therefore they simply adopted the fashion of the activities of the Naga underground movement. Thus, due to the lack of systematic organisation the leaders of the movement were not able to attract the elites of the society of Manipur. Therefore the image of the activities of the Meitei State Committee was not very strong in urban areas.

Whatever the case may be, it is a fact that the outbreak of the Meitei State Committee, as a revolutionary organisation was a landmark in the history of the revolutionary movement of the post-merger period of Manipur. It produced two important impacts on the future history of the state. One is the emergence of the idea of Manipur nationalism and the other is the growth of the political concept of self-determination among the people of the younger generation of the state.

## UNITED NATIONAL LIBERATION FRONT (UNLF) (PRE-R.G.M. PERIOD)

The birth of the United National Liberation Front (UNLF) as a revolutionary organisation was a great landmark in the history of the revolutionary movement of Manipur. The emergence of this organisation gave a new social outlook and political concept, which is quite different from the earlier thought process, to the people particularly the younger generation. The establishment of this organisation was an eye opener on the way of new political and social outlook of the state and their relationship with other people. Although it is not required to go into detail it can be deduced that the birth of this revolutionary organisation was more or less directly or indirectly related with the emerging political, economic and social life which was developed just after integration into India in 1949. To a question an ex-revolutionary leader had categorically stressed that armed revolution was the only solution to the undesirable political and economic development in Manipur and the spirit of the idea of Manipuri nationalism would be the greatest strength and weapon of their revolution. In this respect another ex-revolutionary leader said that the idea of Manipuri nationalism was planted on the fervent soil of Manipur by Sagolsem Indramani Singh of Thangmeiband and Yangmaso Saiza, two great personalities of this state. Their attempt and demand was to remove foreigners from Manipur in the beginning of 1950s. It may be treated as a basic foundation for the growth of the idea of self-determination among the youths of this state. It is a well-known fact that Shri Sagolsem Indramani Singh was the only person in Manipur who devoted all his energy for the strengthening of both physical and moral power of the youths of the state. He thought that the strength and unity of the state would be in the hands of the people of future generation. Therefore, with this objective he made a tireless effort to give proper guidelines to the youths by establishing schools and physical training centres single handedly without the help of the government. Even some prominent ex-members of one of the revolutionary parties regarded him as the only person in Manipur who introduced modern thought and idea among the youths.

There was some confusion about the fixation of the year and date of the establishment of this organisation. R. Constantine wrote "Almost simultaneously but silently men who mean business were getting together. First emerged the Pan-Mongoloid Movement (some insiders deny that the Pan-Mongoloid Movement was not at all there) followed by the United National Liberation Front. The exact date of the origin of this body is disputed but it is generally believed that the movement to establish an independent Manipur began sometime in 1965."[17] and Pan-Manipuri Youth League (PANMYL) was working very effectively on this political line as an overground frontal organisation of the UNLF. He further said that this organisation was formally established at a meeting held at Thangmeiband in the month of November. The meeting was held in the late evening and it was attended by seven members. According to an ex-revolutionary leader, the United Liberation Front was established in the year 1963 at a meeting held at Keishampat. At that time he was not a top ranking leader. According to him nine persons attended the meeting and a pseudo government was formed on that day. Thus, there was some confusion about the exact date of the establishment of this organisation. But in an official paper issued on the twenty-eight birth anniversary it is recorded that the United National Liberation Front (UNLF) was established on the 24th November, 1964.[18] In order to carry on the movement they formed an executive committee of nine members. It is recorded that this committee was the highest policy decision making body of the organisation. All the members of the committee were allotted different portfolios. They were, (1) President, (2) Vice President, (3) General Secretary / Secretary Defence, (4) Foreign Secretary, (5) Home Secretary, (6) Secretary to Foreign Secretary, (7) Secretary War, (8) Secretary Political Affairs, (9) Secretary Publicity and Propaganda. Apart from this there was also another body in the organisation. It was known as Co-ordination Committee and it was constituted by 30 (thirty) members. Kalalu Kamei of Khoupum village was the founder President of this organisation and Thangkhopao Singsheet of Ehang Karong was the founder Vice President.

One of the most important objective of this organisation was to preserve a distinctive national identity and to create a free and wholesome human existence for the people of Manipur.[19] In this respect they had strongly deplored the policy of the India government. They asserted that the decadence in the Manipuri society, the meaningless existence of the peoples, particularly the youth floating in a vacuum, the erosion in the distinctive national identity and the parasitic thinking that they cannot survive without depending on India,[20] were all the creation of the policy of the Indian government. So, they called the present administrative system as "Indian colonial rule". In this regard they had pointed out two points as the main features of the Indian colonial rule i.e., (1) the erosion of the distinctive national identity of the Manipuri, and (2) suppression of their economy as a captive (that is. not allowing Manipur to develop its productive forces) thereby making Manipur permanently dependent on Indian capital (in money forms).[21] Then they concluded that to uproot and to overthrow Indian colonial rule was the only way to the restoration of their national independence. They believed that the only path to achieve this objective was to carry out a "National People's Democratic Revolution".

Then just after the establishment of this revolutionary organisation the leaders were actively engaged in the expansion and strengthening of their position among different peoples and groups. It is said that as an attempt to establish a common objective they even tried to contact the leaders of the Meitei State Committee. But the top leader of the Meitei State Committee was not in favour of the proposal of the leaders of UNLF and so they carried on their revolutionary activities in their own way. This was not the end of UNLF in their effort to form a common front of all the different groups of people in Manipur. In order to mobilise among the tribal people, the organization gave the responsibility to Thangkhopao Singsheet. Chief of Ehang Karong village. He was a great and true nationalist. He always said that no revolution could be successfully launched without co-operation and understanding between Meiteis and peoples of surrounding hill areas. But unfortunately he was killed by some unidentified persons. Before his death, as an important representative of the UNLF, he met Laldenga, the leader of Mizo. It is said that he was able to bring a positive understanding between the two organisations and Laldenga even assured him of sending their General Secretary to Manipur for further discussion. But for the reason which was not known to anybody the points of understanding were not materialised. Another important tribal leader of the UNLF was Lalkhohen. His only dream was to establish 'a greater Manipur'. It is mentioned that Lalkhohen was a man of action. He always prefered quick action. But his desire was not applicable at the moment. So. later on he joined hands with Laldenga along with some tribal volunteers of UNLF. Thus the leaders of the UNLF have made a serious and sincere attempt to bring all the different groups of people under the banner of this organisation for liberation.

After having a full ideological preparation the leadership of UNLF decided to take help from other foreign powers. First they selected the

Chinese government. The reason of their preference to this country perhaps was influenced by the ideological difference between China and India. On the basis of this idea they thought that they would be able to launch a successful revolution with the help and co-operation of the Chinese government. With this intention first they tried to contact the officials of the Chinese Embassy in Delhi through a Cambodian student who studied in Delhi University. His name was Rev. Pen Sawen. It is said that he was a volunteer of Vietminh guerrilla. But the Chinese Embassy did not give any reply to their request. They made several attempts to get a response. But all their efforts ended without any result. Then they decied to go to Pakistan. The organisation entrusted the responsibility of going to East Pakistan to Oinam Sudhirkumar Singh, another leader of the organisation. It is said that at that time Sudhir had a relative in East Pakistan. His name was Oinam Mikoi Singh. Through him Sudhir had enjoyed the privilege of going to East Pakistan very frequently. Before going to East Pakistan, the UNLF, through Sudhir contacted Oinam Mikoi and requested him to establish a contact point with the Government of Pakistan. After getting the information from that man some important leaders of UNLF including Sudhir went to Pakistan. But they were arrested at the railway station. After giving a detailed information about the purpose of their visit to Pakistan, the local official informed the foreign office which treated them as their guests and they were brought to Dacca. In Dacca they met some important persons of the government of Pakistan and they expressed their desire to get help from them. The concerned person of the Pakistan government listened carefully. But without giving any reason they expressed their inability to extend their co-operation to UNLF. It is observed that they, perhaps, were very busy as they were also actively monitoring the process of the tide of the war between Egypt and Israel. Then they left Pakistan and they were escorted by the security personnel of Pakistan up to the border area. Then they again entered into Pakistan to meet the officials of the Chinese embassy. But on the way they were arrested at the Bhanughat railway station in Pakistan. They were brought to Sylhet. They explained to the local police about the purpose of their visit to East Pakistan. It is further said that from there O. Sudhir with some persons went to Dacca to meet the Consulate of Chinese Government. But the Chinese officials did not express their opinion openly. Thus their mission was abruptly ended without any positive result.

In the meantime, in the year 1968, a rift was developed inside the rank and file of the organisation of the United National Liberation Front. An official record mentioned that the rift was due to the differences in the policy and programme of the organisation. However some ex-revolutionary members said that the rift was mainly due to the leadership crisis. On the other hand other members squarely put the responsibility of the split of the organisation to O. Sudhirkumar Singh. It is mentioned that his attempt to control the party was the main cause of the split. At that time he was the Foreign Secretary and by virtue of this position the party entrusted the responsibility of the contact with the officials of East Pakistan to him. Then after getting the opportunity of getting help from that country, Sudhir went to Pakistan with some of his followers without giving information to the higher authority of the party in the beginning of 1969. This was the main cause of the split.[22] Another prominent ex-revolutionary leader made an attempt to establish the causes of the split of the UNLF mainly as a result of the class difference among the rank and file of the leadership. He strongly emphasised that the conflict between the middle class leadership group and the proletariat group was the main reason for the split. Secondly, he also admitted that the negative attitude of the Pakistan government was mainly due to the lack of the demonstration of the military activities of the organisation. Such type of position was not desirable to the younger group of the organisation. This issue was another unavoidable important reason for the growth of dissatisfaction among the younger members. Then a group of young persons under the leadership of O. Sudhirkuamr Singh went to East Pakistan. This development, in fact, marked the end of the activities of the 'first phase' of the United National Liberation Front. Thus, without giving any concrete demonstration about their existence to the common people the life of the organisation was temporarily closed with the split of party.

## REVOLUTIONARY GOVERNMENT OF MANIPUR (RGM)

The establishment of the 'Revolutionary Government of Manipur under the leadership of Oinam Sudhirkumar Singh may be regarded as one of the important milestones in the history of the revolutionary movements in Manipur. As has been mentioned above due to the difference of opinions among the rank and file particularly in the nature of the working of the organisation a large chunk of revolutionary members came out from the UNLF under the leadership of Sudhirkumar and formed another revolutionary organisation known as 'Revolutionary Government of Manipur' (RGM). The most important aspect of this organisation was that it gave certain positive impact in the thought process of the social, political and economic life of the common people. Apart from this they were also able to change even the attitude and the political outlook of the leaders of the Central Government of India. After having such a new type of unexpected experience the Indian Government began to give a serious thought and importance to the real problem in the grievances of the people of Manipur.

It is said that before the establishment of this revolutionary organization, O. Sudhirkumar Singh made an attempt to bring together some organisations like the 'South Eastern People's Organisation' (SEPO) of Thoubal, the 'Kaibiron' and some other small organisations under the single roof of an ideologica. umbrella. His aim was to establish a federal government and on the basis of this objective he made a proposal for the establishment of the 'South-East Asian Hill Region Mongolian Integrated Federal Republic'.[23] In order to materialize his objective he tried to meet a large number of tribal leaders of different sections. Then at his initiative the 'Consolidation Committee' (CONSOCOM) was formed. The objective of this Committee was to bring all the like-minded organisations under the banner of a common committee. The other members were, (1) Nameirakpam Bisheshwor Singh, (2) R.K. Sanajaoba, and (3) W. Sanatomba Singh.[24] In order to have an effective administrative activities, the body of the 'Committee' had constituted seven departments. They were (1) Director of Foreign Affairs, (2) Director of Intelligence Affairs, (3) Director of Finance, (4) Director of Home Affairs, (5) Director of Defence, (6) Director of Publicity, and (7) Director of Food and Communication.[25]

Then after having a brief preparatory work they have decided to send volunteers to East Pakistan (now Bangladesh). But it is not very clear whether the decision of sending volunteers for getting arm training from the East Pakistan was made after having full understanding with Pakistani government or not. From the future course of action it seems that this issue was not clear. It is said that although Sudhir went to Pakistan under the UNLF banner, he tried to contact the Pakistani authorities under a different banner. With his sharp organisational skill, Sudhir developed links with the Pakistan authorities".[26] But the practical experience which the volunteers had come across at the time of entering Pakistan is to be analysed. A big question may be put on the issue of the integrity and maturity of relationship and understanding between the government of Pakistan and leaders of the organisation. Whatever the case may be they began to send the volunteers after taking a final decision at a meeting held at Kakwa, a place situated at south Imphal.[27] And the responsibility of the sending of volunteers from Manipur to East Pakistan was left with N. Bisheshwor Singh.[28] Now, Sudhir was fully convinced that it would not be possible to seek help from Pakistan without an organisation. So, he set up the 'Revolutionary Government of Manipur' (RGM) at Sylhet in the year 1969.[29] From this fact it is quite clear that the decision of the sending of volunteers was made without proper understanding with the Pakistan government. It seems that everything was arranged by Sudhir on the basis of his personal capabilities. This was also a very important reason for having a lot of shortcomings in their movement. Such type of decision was regarded by R. Constantine as a 'potentially the most dangerous step......... for the young stormy petals.'[30] The first batch of seven members left Imphal for Pakistan in May 1969 and out of this two persons were involved in the Imphal College robbery.[31] An official record mentioned that the volunteers of the revolutionary party left Imphal for East Pakistan on the 21st May, 1969.[32] However, the records did not mention the exact number of members. On the other hand it is also mentioned that the number of volunteers who entered into the area of East Pakistan were 200 two hundred and after crossing the international boundary they landed at Bhanughat in Sylhet where they met their leaders.[33] It is further said that soon after their arrival an internal wrangling cropped up and they began to blame one another for bringing a larger number of persons to Pakistan without valid documents,[34] that too before establishment of a solid and firm relationship with the Pakistani authority. From this evidences it can be suggested that the whole planning of the organisation was not properly done with the full understanding among the rank and file of the party.

Their miscalculation had created a serious problem and the misunderstanding immediately came out on the visible surface when their volunteers were arrested by the Pakistan police. In this respect it is observed that "Pakistan authorities might have thought that helping Meitei extremists might become the cause for direct confrontation with the Indian army at this border area".[35] This observation cannot be completely ruled out as the situation had strongly demanded for such action because at that time a serious strained relationship was developed between Pakistan and India. Pakistan had a strong desire to ease the situation. Accordingly, Pakistan police kept all the arrested Meitei volunteers in the Maulvi Bazar Jail. It is recorded that on the 1st of July the Manipuri youths were arrested by the Pakistan Police at Bhanubil and from there they were brought to Kamalganj Thana. That day they were kept in a Dak Bungalow near the police station and the next day they were shifted to the Moulvi Bazar Police Station and produced them before the Sub-Divisional Officer (SDO) of that circle. Then they were sent to the jail.[36] On the 16th July, twenty-six volunteers were transferred to Sylhet Jail and after two days another batch of twenty-six youths were sent in the same jail. On the 30th July all the revolutionary volunteers, except their leader, O. Sudhirkumar had been taken by the East Pakistan Rifle (EPR) to a tea garden and asked them to go back to India. But since they were not able to know the roads they again came back to the tea estate and they were again kept under the care of the personnel of East Pakistan Rifle in the Kamalganj Police Station. On the night of 31st July they were again taken by the East Pakistan Rifle to the border area and asked them to go back to India. They warned them not to come back again otherwise they would be shot dead by the army. From this area they were divided into several groups and began to enter into India from different directions. It is said that while crossing 'Manu' some Manipuri youths were arrested by the Kalishhar Police and some by the Dharmanagar Police. An official record says that during the period between 1st to 6th August, 1969, fifty-six Manipuri youths were arrested in Tripura, thirty-four within Kailashhar Police Station and remaining twenty-two within Dharmanagar Police station.[37] In a petition filed to Court of the Hon'ble Chief Justice of the Supreme Court of India, the petitioner, Moirangthem Tomchou Singh, Deputy Superintendent of Police (Prosecution) of the Government of Manipur affirmed that the arrested

Manipuri youths were all revolutionaries "who had gone to East Pakistan to receive training in arms for the purpose of overthrowing the Government of Manipur by armed revolution with a view to making Manipur a sovereign state outside Indian Union."[38]

It is reported that Oinam Sudhirkumar, after the deportation of the volunteers to the border area of Tripura, had sneaked into the Moulvi Bazar and there he met other eight members who had secretly avoided the crossing over to Indian territories. He then went to Dacca, the capital of East Pakistan, where he successfully met the high ranking military officers of Pakistan. After this meeting they began to give special attention to the Manipuri youths and arms training were given to the eight Manipuri youths at 'Borlekha Commando Training Centre[39] in Sylhet District. The training was continued for two years. In the meantime Indo-Pak War broke out in 1971 and it gave a serious set back to the moral of the revolutionary youths of Manipur. Then they crossed the border areas and on the way back to Manipur they had several encounters with the Indian army. Asem Indra Singh was killed and then with the help of villagers they tried to enter into Manipur from the Jiri area. While they were in the jungle of Lakhisona they were surrounded by the CRPF personals and an exchange of fire took place between them. Then they escaped to Jiribam area and from there they tried to enter into the valley area of Manipur. But unfortunately they were arrested at Nungba on the National Highway No. 53. With this arrest the activities of the RGM virtually came to an end and all the arrested revolutionaries were put inside the police custody for interrogation by a local magistrate.

All the arrested persons gave their statement to the police under section 161 of the Code of Criminal Procedure.[40] After getting the statement from the arrested persons the Circle Inspector Police of Lamphel Police Station who dealt with these cases, submitted a report on August 8, 1969 to the higher authority of the Government of Manipur. In the report the Circle Inspector categorically pointed out the real objective of the volunteers. It is said that "........... about 300 Manipuri youths including Arambam Somarendra Singh, Oinam Sudhir Singh, R.K. Sanajaoba, W. Sanatomba Singh, I. Kunje Singh had conspired together since January 1969 in Imphal and elsewhere to organise groups of youths with unlicensed arms and explosive in every part of Manipur with a view to attack persons and damage public and government properties. to commit robbery, dacoity and arson. to drive out non Manipuris. to attack government servants. security forces and create disorder in Manipur."[41] The report further mentioned that the purpose of their visit to East Pakistan was for the establishment of a conspiracy to overthrow the Manipur government and to make it a sovereign state outside the Indian Union.[42] The report also gave an adverse remark about their activities in which it is said that in order to achieve their objective they entered into conspiracy to commit robberies and decoities for raising funds.[43] Thus the historic attempt of the revolutionary volunteers of R.G.M. for the establishment of a sovereign indepeindent Manipur came to an end without having any achievement.

Nevertheless the attempt of the leaders of R.G.M. for the consolidation of their activities cannot be brushed aside easily. They were fully aware that the success of their attempt lies in the capacity of the raising of funds. With this objective they also made a vigorous efforts to raise funds from different levels. An ex-member revealed that at the beginning each and every member of the organisation had contributed ten paise weekly to the part fund. Apart from this, they also tried to raise funds by adopting different methods. On the 15th May, 1969 at about 12 :30 p.m. the volunteers of R.G.M. had robbed Rs. 10,000 (Ten thousand) from the two employees of Imphal College. This money was for the distribution to the students of the low income group.[44] In his confessional statement, M. Irabot Singh said that "one Brajamani Singh got the expenditure money from the organisation, Khomdon, Kunje, Nabachandra, and Dhaneshor robbed money from Imphal College office for the organisation."[45] On the 18th February, 1969 at about 4. p.m. two person looted money from the Imphal Branch Post office. The exact amount of money was not known.[46] In his confessional statement, Phurailatpam Toto Sharma disclosed everything about the activities of R.G.M. particularly about the system of the raising of funds. According to his statement the decision for the raising of fund was discussed in a meeting held in the month of July, 1969 at the residence of Salam Shayananda Singh of Kwakeithel Maning, Imphal. About 20 persons attended the meeting. Some important members who attended the meeting were. 1. Meisnam Biren Singh of Maipo Leirak, 2. Saikhom Jugolchandra Singh of Salam Leikai, 3. R.K. Sanajaoba of Singjamei Leisangthem Leikai. 4.

Nameirakpam Kumar Singh of Naorem Leikai. 5. Salam Shyamananda Singh of Kwakeithel Maning.[47] In order to meet the expenditure they decided to rob the bank and some other big financial establishments. For this purpose they procured some small fire arms. They looted Rs. 5160.50 (Five thousand, one hundred and sixty and fifty paise) from Life Insurance Corporation and it was followed by the robbery at Ibencha High School and from the shop of Murli Agrawal, etc.

Indeed, the statement of Toto Sharma who was the respondent No. 18 of the case between the Union Territory of Manipur and Yumnam Biren Singh and others was a great irreparable set back to the moral of the volunteers of this organisation. Apart from the issue of raising funds, he also disclosed many unknown facts about the organisational structure of R.G.M. to the informer of the police. In this respect R. Constantine mentioned the connection between Toto Sharma and one constable of Special Intelligence Bureau (SIB).[48] It is also said that after getting information about his suspicious activities, Toto was forced to leave the team at Jiri before entering East Pakistan.[49]

Meanwhile the Manipur Government began to arrest a large number of R.G.M. activists including some top leaders. According to a press release the Manipur Police Department arrested the following leaders, viz., (1) Bonbihari Singh, External Affairs Minister, (2) Brajamani Singh, Home Affairs, (3) Jugol Singh, Internal Affairs, (4) Hemba Singh, Information and Publicity, (5) Ingobi Singh, Deputy Director, External Affairs.[50] Another significant achievement of the Police was the arrest of N. Pahari Singh who was the Chief of the Army Staff of the Manipuri Revolutonary.[51] But it is not very clear whether he was a revolutionary member of the R.G.M. or not. It is reported that when he was arrested the police was able to collect a lot of valuable papers which dealt with High Commissioner of Pakistan.[52] The arrest of these people was followed by the mass arrest of R.G.M. volunteers by the police. In the middle of November, 1969 the police arrested 123 volunteers.[53]

Such mass arrest of volunteers severely demoralised and disheartened other enthusiastic revolutionaries who had strongly believed that their armed venture would show a quick positive result. The outbreak of liberation movement in East Pakistan had completely smashed their plan to take a maximum help from Pakistan. Then without having any alternative some of them surrendered to the government. The most important dramatic turn in the minds of some of the volunteers was that just after the announcement of the Statehood, twenty-three volunteers in the Imphal Jail requested the Lt. Governor of Manipur to set them free. In their application they categorically mentioned that in the future they would not go in this path. They said "................ we never think of it, and we shall never do it. If there is a suspicion upon us at all we may be kept under the police supervision for a certain period of time."[54] They also sent copies to the local newspapers and Chairman of the All Parties Statehood Demand Co-ordinating body. The copy was received by the Convener on 19th October, 1970. Then with the arrest of all the key leaders of the organization, the highly enthusiastic activities of the Revolutionary Government of Manipur (R.G.M.) came to an end and normalcy was restored gradually in Manipur particularly in Imphal valley. Then with the coming of new ministry after statehood, a general amnesty was declared to all the revolutionary volunteers. It is mentioned that a sizeable section of extremist youths showed remarkable interest towards the overground politics.[55]

Many opinions were advanced in regard to the failure of the organisation. The biggest tragedy of the reason of the failure of R.G.M. lies in the ideological front. It is alleged that the political ideology of R.G.M. is based on the Meitei fanaticism, the Meitei nationalist chauvinism,[56] etc. But this allegation is not properly spelled out with distinctive empirical evidence. Some were of the view that the weak organisational structure, lack of ideological commitment among the volunteers and absence of expected help from Pakistan also played a major role in the failure of the activities of the organisation. In this respect it can be suggested that the attainment of full-fledged state of Manipur was also a big cause for the failure of the movement. It is a fact that people were not happy in the manner in which Manipur had integrated into India. People were also fed up with the changing political development in the state from the year 1949. Therefore, they felt that their political and economic hardship would be solved only when Manipur got statehood. Accordingly the minds of the majority of the people of Manipur were fully concentrating on the agitation for statehood. So, when the Central Government gave a green signal for statehood the people were so happy and they even thought that it was a great relief from any type of undesirable political activities. Even the people who gave loyalty to the cause of R.G.M. had returned to the main route of Indian nationalism the moment Manipur got statehood. In this connection, R. Constantine rightly observed that the "RGM lost its raison d'eter with full statehood and was left high and dry."[57] In the official report of 1972-73 the Government of Manipur mentioned that the Revolutionary Government of Manipur which was in touch with many countries and which had considerable following had been virtually smashed in the year 1970-71 and finally became extinct in the year 1971-72. They were badly ruoted by the police.

## PEOPLE'S LIBERATION ARMY UNIT (EASTERN REGION) (1978-1981)

The establishment of the People's Liberation Army (Eastern Region) as an armed revolutionary organisation was also another significant development in the historical process of the armed revolutionary movements in Manipur and also in the history of the North-Eastern Region of the Indian Union. This revolutionary organisation was established on the 25th September, 1978 at Nongpok Sekmai.[58] The biggest asset of this organisation was its ideology. It strongly emphasized for the establishment of a classless society based on the principle of Marxism. This ideological aspect was a distinctive departure from the ideological concept of the previous revolutionary organisations. At the same time, the main objective of the organisation was to establish a distinctive separate political identity of the entire states of North-Eastern Region outside the Indian Union. Therefore, the operational areas of P.L.A. had covered all the states of this region. In his speech of 25th September, 1979 the leader of the party N. Bisheshwor Singh said that the aim of the organisation was to carry out two important objectives. The first one was "to organise revolutionary front in the group level, covering the area of Manipur (Kangleipak), Nagaland, Mizoram, Assam, Tripura, Meghalaya and Arunachal Pradesh."[59] In order to translate their objective into action they placed its general and specific programme for discussion in the first plenary session of the "Revolutionary People's Front". He said that the sole objective of this organisation was to launch a movement of the similar type of 'Nanchang Uprising', a famous historic revolutionary uprising in the Chinese revolution led by Chou-En-Lai, in this region. He coined the PLA movement as the "Second Nanchang Uprising."[60] Thus, under the banner of this objective and principle the People's Liberation Army (Eastern Unit) was established.

As has already been mentioned above, just after the establishment of a full-fledged state the new ministry had declared a general amnesty to all the revolutionary volunteers. Accordingly all the leaders and activists who were inside the jail were released without any condition and they were given an opportunity to start a new life within the framework of the Indian Constitution. The rehabilitation programme was also initiated by the government. Then some ex-revolutionaries under the initiative of Late O. Sudhirkumar and Bisheshwor had started a 'Co-operative Society' near Moreh, a border town of Manipur. However, the actual name of the society cannot be ascertained. According to the information of an ex-revolutionary, the name of the society was 'Ideal Multipurpose Co-operative Society'.[61] The official paper of the government mentioned that the name of the society was "Kangleipak Agro Multipurpose Society"[62]. It is recorded that the society was established in October 1975 with a meeting held at the residence of Salam Shyamananda Singh.[63] About 14 to15 persons were present and Shyamananda was the president of the society. They requested the Chief Minister of Manipur to allot an area of 280 acres of land at Haolok. They tried to get the area till 1976 but for reason which was not known to anybody they were not able to get it. However, Sudhirkumar and his party could get an area of 0.40 acres of land near 'Khudengthabi' in Tengnoupal District. The other members were not happy at the attitude of Sudhirkumar and so the idea of the society was dropped along with the new proposal for 'Kangleipak Yaipha Thousikol', which aimed to develope handloom and small scale industry.[64] It is said that the 'Co-operative Society' was established at Kondon Lairembi in Chandel District with an objective to give settlement to those persons, particularly Meitei people, who came from Tripura, Cachar, Burma, Assam and East Pakistan (Now Bangladesh). But O. Sudhirkumar had shifted it to Khudengthabi and destroyed its purpose.[65] Whatever the case may be it is an undeniable fact that the real motive of the organisers behind this co-operative venture might be to reorganise their splintered groups to renew the armed movement. It is also said that the objective of the society was to reorganise the armed movement.[66] This was also clearly evident from the later actions of the ex-leaders of the then R.G.M., particularly N. Bisheshwor Singh.

Meanwhile a serious difference was developed in the policy and programme between Sudhirkumar and Bisheshwor. It is said that Sudhirkumar and his party wanted to remain as a silent observer until a favourable political atmosphere emerged in the state. Whereas Bisheshwor and his group believed that their aim for the establishment of a sovereign state would die out if they did not continue the movement. It is also said that Sudhirkumar was very much in favour of taking help from U.S.A. whereas Bisheshwor was in favour of China. He did not have confidence in the integrity of the U.S.A.[67] Because of this difference Bisheshwor made up his mind for the establishment of another revolutionary organisation. He also said that before he left for Lasha he met Samarendra and disclosed his plan.[68] However, he refused to disclose anything about the response of his one time leader. In regard to the objective of the establishment of a new revolutionary organisation, he said that the objective of the proposed organisation was to build up a strong party which represents the whole nationalities and the interest of the broad masses."[69] He further said, "R.G.M. cannot meet the present situation and fails to serve the interest of the workers and peasants, as its political line is wrong and therefore fails to represent the interest of the majority of our people and our whole nationalities."[70] Therefore on the ground of these points he had clarified that he had dissolved the ten years old R.G.M.[71] He also strongly stressed the immediate need for a strong and well disciplined party so that it could represent the interest of the broad masses, the workers and peasants and the whole nationalities.

With this objective and in order to establish a well disciplined party in the near future Bisheshwor left Manipur for Lasha in the year 1976 along with 15 youths.[72] The official report of the government mentioned that Nameirakpam Bisheshwor Singh with sixteen volunteers went to Lasha (Tibet) via Gorakpur and Nepal in April, 1976.[73] However, according to an information the number of persons who went to China were twenty including the leader Bisheshwor. The other members were (1) Kabichandra alias Langlen, Koirou, (2) Indrajit alias Yaima, (3) N. Nilamani, (4) Biramangol alias Ibohal, (5) N. Rajen Achouba alias Mera, (6) Chirom Ranjit Singh alias Nongyai,

(7) Rajen Macha alias Koba, (8) S. Temba alias Ningthou, (9) Thoudam Kunjabihari alias Raghu, (10) Manikanta, (11) Chaobhal alias Koirou, (12) W. Brojen Singh, (13) Amumacha, (14) Kh. Khaba alias Nilakomol, (15) N. Thoiba, (16) Loya, (17) Surjaboro alias Khamba, Shanta, (18) Chaoba alias Koiren, (19) Kulla Koirou, etc.[74]

Thus after facing a lot of problems and difficulties these revolutionary volunteers were able to get armed training from China along with the ideological principle of Marxism and thought of Mao-Tse-Tung. However, it is said that though they got training from the Chinese government, they were not fully satisfied with the nature of the Chinese government. Particularly, the leader of the team, N. Bisheshwor Singh, was not happy with the dictatorial attitude of China. Actually he did not like to go at the dictation of China.[75] It is said that every month the Chinese officials showed the expenditure incurred by the Chinese government for them. Bisheshwor was not happy with this. Apart from this, they also put a condition that at the end of every month, they should submit a report of their activities to the Chinese Government. Seeing this highly provocative nature of the Chinese authority, Bisheshwor thought that if they go according to their dictation they would not be able to get recognition of other countries.[76] So, after getting training all of them came back without taking even a single material help like fire arms, guns, etc. from China. It is said that they returned from China with sword, dao and iron rode.[77] Then they reached Dimapur in Nagaland. All of them had stayed there for three months by doing all sorts of available physical works. But three members were not able to follow the order of the leader and they came back to Manipur. So, later on these three persons were not given any type of assignment in the organisation. Bisheshwor said that it was a kind of primary training given to the members of his organisation.[78]

As was stated above, the objective of the People's Liberation Army (Eastern Unit) was for the establishment of a distinctive separate political identity of the different states of North-Eastern Region of India. It is also mentioned that Bisheshwor strongly believed that the idea for having a separate independent political identity of Manipur would not be practicable. So he embraced the idea of regionalism.[79] Bisheshwor also justified his stand by saying that he applied Marxism in his approach purely from the concept of the totality of North-East.[80]

He further said that if it was for Manipur. Marxism cannot be applicable because the society of Manipur is built up on the basis of a strong kinship relationship. Thus, on this basis. People's Liberation Army (Eastern Unit) was established for having a separate political identity of the people of North-Eastern Region of the Indian Union. This revolutionary organisation was started with a small apex body i.e.. the 'Executive Body'. It was constituted by seven members and Bisheshwor was the Chairman. This body was the only decision making body. The members were 1. Shri N. Bisheshwor Singh (Chairman). 2. Biramangol. 3. Temba, 4. Chirom Ranjit, 5. Rajen Achouba, 6. Rajen Macha. 7. Kabichandra,[81] and most of the work of foreign affaires was dealt with by Biramangol. With the formation of this body the PLA began to strengthen the organisation, and membership drive also had started.

There was no restriction on the enrolment of members. Any person of any religion can be a member of this orgnisation. But certain special privilege was given to those persons who migrated from Burma, Bangladesh or others. The selection of membership was made on the basis of three criteria, i.e., "First, his or her class origin. Second, ideological consciousness which decides his or her full membership and third, his or her loyalty to the cause of the revolution."[82] According to the procedure, the person who intended to become the member of the organisation should be introduced to the head of the body by either one or two 'full members' by submitting a complete bio-data of the person. And if he or she was found eligible, a forwarding letter should be sent by his or her guardian by requesting to enroll their son or daughter as a member of the organisation.[83] Then it was followed by an oath-taking ceremony before the head of the party. After the completion of these procedures he can be an extra-ordinary member of the party. The membership of the party had two categories, one was full member and another was extra-ordinary member. The extra-ordinary member was a temporary member who was on probation period. One may become the full time membership only when he was able to pass all the tests given by the party. The period of training was also different according to their class to which they belong. For persons who belong to working class. it was six months and for persons in the peasant class it was nine months.[84] It is also mentioned that "The strata or class will be tested for an indefinite period of time."[85] As a matter of policy the party, in its initial step, gave emphasis only on the working and peasant class. The policy of the party was categorically pointed out by Bisheshwor in his speech of 25th February, 1979. He said, "Our cadres should be selected from those section of people who earn livelihood by selling their labour, power and their two hands, be carefully checked their class origin and their ideological consciousness".[86]

The strong ideological foundation was an important feature of People's Liberation Army Unit (Eastern Region). As has been mentioned above, the ideological foundation of P.L.A. was based on the principle of 'Marxism'. They strongly emphasised that the P.L.A. was not the enemy of the Indian people. All the Indian working class group was taken by the members of P.L.A. as their friends. But they were strongly against the bureaucratic government of India. They said that their policy was an open door policy. They welcomed all the patriots, moderates who opposed the Delhi regime. In a speech of the party meeting held on 25th September 1978, N. Bisheshwor Singh said "it is also clear that we are internationalists and we unite with international proletariats which comprise the majority of the world population."[87] The ideological principle of P.L.A. was to continue with new 'democratic revolution'[88] based on armed struggle. They also believed that their ideological aim could be successfully materialised only when there was a unity of all the different communities like Naga, Mizos, Kukis, Meiteis, etc. whom they regarded as different 'nationalities".[89] They also condemned the theory of "Meitei for Meiteis, Mizo for Mizos, Naga for Nagas.' This idea was regarded by PLA as a reactionary theory and they took it as a great cause for the failure of their revolution. The members of this revolutionary organisation were fully convinced that war could be eliminated or removed only by war. They had strongly asserted that 'war is the highest form of strength for resolving contradiction'. Therefore the repressive measure of the central government was regarded by the People's Liberation Army (Eastern Unit) as work of counter revolutionary war. Therefore, they claimed that counter revolutionary war of the enemy can never be defeated by any means of peace or others but only 'by the war of the people.' In a message to his party comrade N. Bisheshwor Singh said, their enemy (Delhi government) possessed two hands 'one is suppressive and the other deceptive.' This attitude should be exposed through all kinds of means. He suggested that the moral of the people should be raised by 'educating and helping them through education and oragnisation and built up a firm revolutionary mass base'.[90] He further said that no revolution could be successful without the mass base and so he asked his comrades to have confidence in the strength of the people. The members of the PLA valued the revolutionary principle of their organisation. They were of the opinion that this principle should not be sold out to the enemy at any cost and the only objective of a real revolutionary was to persist in armed fighting till victory was achieved. In short the workers and peasants should take the leading role in their revolution. However, they also realised the importance of intellectuals in the ongoing process of the revolution. They said that no revolution could be successful without the participation of revolutionary intellectuals. But according to them intellectuals cannot lead the revolution until they were re-educated by the objective realities and adopt the hardship of revolution by transforming their nature of subjectivism.[91] The PLA thought that the intellectuals, though they possess the quality of analytical technique on every issue, cannot go to the broad masses particularly to the workers and peasants. According to their observation the personal interest, such as fame, is more important to the intellectual than the sacrifice and so they always have the habitual nature of capitulation to the enemy particularly when they meet some temporary defeats.[92] On the basis of this observation N. Bisheshwor, in his speech on the 25th September, 1978, strongly asserted that peasants located area should be the revolutionary base of their organisation. They would be able to destroy the effecting strength of the enemy only when the rural and village areas are transformed into a strong fortified base area. He further said that the PLA (Eastern Region) would be able to liberate the people from the colonial rule of Delhi government only when their strength was completely destroyed.[93]

On the basic foundation of this ideological principles the People's Liberation Army (PLA) (Eastern Region) began to start their revolutionary activities very effectively. On June 29, 1978 the PLA activities shot a Jamandar of Manipur Rifles and his 9 m.m.(Nine m.m.) pistol was snatched away by them. This particular incident was regarded as the first revolutionary action of this organisation.[94] On the 29th July, 1978 they shot down one sepoy of Manipur Rifles near

Dharmasala in the heart of Imphal city and took his gun.[95] Then on 17th of July, 1978 two police personnels were shot death at Takhel Leikai at Tiddim Road by the volunteers of PLA and made away with a 9 m.m. pistol.[96] Two days later, i.e. on 19th July, 1978 two sepoys of Manipur Rifles were killed at Wangjing and a one sten gun, two rifles and some ammunitions were taken away by them.[97] Thus, the leaders and volunteers of People's Liberation Army (Eastern Unit) began to campaign their activities very successfully.

The 14th January, 1979 was an important day in the course of the revolutionary activities of PLA (Eastern Region). On this very day the volunteers of this organisation killed O. Sudhirkumar Singh who was a leader of RGM (Revolutionary Government of Manipur) along with his two associates. The assassination of Sudhirkumar was regarded by PLA as a great achievement in their activities. By giving justification to their action the PLA leader regarded the group of Sudhirkumar as "a gang of counter revolutionaries who become hostile to the people who love revolution."[98] They claimed that this gang was set up with an armed support of both Central and State Governments to destroy people's revolutionary force. They further alleged that O. Sudhirkumar and his followers had committed a lot of reactionary actions by arresting and torturing the innocent people particularly of Singjamei area and by forcibly collecting money from different parts of Manipur by pretending that he was a revolutionary.[100] They further said that in April 1976 Shri Sudhirkumar and his group made a veined attempt to track down their (PLA) mission to China.[101] On the basis of these allegations and as a matter of principle in handling the counter revolutionary activities, the decision for the removal of Sudhir Kumar's group was adopted on the 11th January 1979.[102] Accordingly, on Sunday, the 14th January 1979, at 9:15 a.m. Sudhirkumar was shot dead by Surjaboro alias Khamba,[103] a Lhasa trained PLA leader along with one R.K. Sanajaoba Singh and Keisham Indra at Singjamei. R.K. Sanajaoba Singh was the elder brother of Smt. Thanilsana Devi, the first wife of N. Bisheshwor Singh. In the words of PLA, "The smashing of the Sudhir's Gang forecasts a bright prospect in the annals of the history of our revolution."[104] And they regarded it as a great success of their party and people.[105]

The killing of four sepoys of Border Security Force on the 26th April, 1979 at Dharmasala in the heart of the Imphal city was another major revolutionary campaign of People's Liberation Army (Eastern Unit). In a press note issued on April 26, 1979 the PLA (Eastern Region) admitted that the killing of four sepoys of B.S.F. at 3:20 p.m. was the work of their revolutionary organisation.[106] They had collected one G.S.L.R., one rifle and two type of sten-guns from the sepoys and escaped from the spot in a jeep along with some hand grenades and small arms.[107] The PLA said that their action was purely for the sake of their motherland[108] and they performed this action under the guidance and leadership of N. Bisheshwor. At the same time they also praised those common people who extended help to the volunteers when they had got an accident on the way to their escape rout.[109] From these activities it can be observed that the revolutionary campaign of PLA might be with two objectives i.e., first, to popularise the existence of this organisation among the people and to create an impression that their organisation was the only revolutionary party which can give a new social and political order in the state, and second, to collect arms and ammunition from the security personals and military camps in order to strengthen their position. The armed movement of PLA (Eastern Region) became a great concern to the government, specially to the state government of Manipur. They also prepared to give a repressive measure against its revolutionary activities. As a first step they tried to check the action of some of the leaders of this organisation by declaring a cash award of Rs. 25,000/- (twenty-five thousand) on their heads.[110] The names of some prominent leaders were 1. Chirom Ranjit Singh, 2. Rajen Achouba, 3. Temba, 4. Surjaboro, 5. Th. Kunjabihari, etc.[111] The official announcement further classified the rewards into three categories, i.e., Rs. 20,000 (Twenty thousand) to the informers who could give information on the whereabouts of the leaders, Rs. 25,000 (Twenty five thousand) on the capture alive and Rs. 20,000 (Twenty thousand) on the capture death.[112] In the midst of this repressive measures, the PLA also began to launch a revolutionary propaganda by putting up the 'Red Star' models in different places particularly in the urban areas of the state. Thus, they were able to penetrate into the midst of common people of the state. On the evening of 9th May, 1979 they distributed a pamphlet in the heart of Imphal city wherein they made an announcement of a new revolutionary method of their organisation and they also gave another information about the establishment of a battalion of army wing.[113] The rescue of Thongam

Kabichandra Singh, a Lasha trained PLA leader who was arrested by the security personnel of the State on the 17th July, 1978 from Heibong Makhong, Mayang Imphal, by the volunteers was also another achievement of this organisation. On the 27th August 1979, at about 11:30 a.m. he was brought in the police van to the Court of Session at Cheirap Court. While the police party was inside the Court compound the cadres of PLA (Eastern Region) attacked the police personnel and they escaped with Kabichandra Singh. In this attack one policeman was killed and four others were injured. All these drama happened within a short duration of fifteen minutes. The common people took it as a wonderful achievement of PLA (Eastern Region) and thus leaders and cadres of this organisation were able to create a very good impression about their activities in the minds of the general public.

The attack on the heavily guarded headquarters of S.S.B. at Mongsangei, about 5 k.m. south-west of Imphal, was also an important military achievement of PLA Unit (Eastern Region). It happened on the night of the 22nd September, 1980. The exchange of fire took place for about one hour and three armed personnel of SSB were killed and another three were injured. It is reported that in this attack the PLA was able to collect seven rifles and one L.M.G. The number of casualties on the side of the organisation was not reported. So, the successful attack on the post of security personnel without any casualties on their side was regarded by the common people as a grand achievement and they began to think that this organisation would be able to bring a separate political identity of Manipur outside the Indian Union. Thus the PLA (Eastern Region) made a continuous armed campaign against the security personnel of the government which they called as 'Delhi Bandits"[114]. In the meantime the government also adopted various types of repressive measures like combing operations by the army personnel in selected places and areas, which they felt were sensitive and necessary. As a result of this, there were a lot of serious disturbances in the peaceful life, particularly among the common people. Shooting, killing and torturing became an order of the daily life of the people of Manipur. On the other hand the army and security personnel also tried to detect the movement of the members of the organisation by stepping up their patrolling activities. Many outposts were opened in sensitive areas and regular checking were conducted and they did not spare even the women, girls and children. Thus the common people began to face a serious insecurity problem in their life.

Another major military activity of the People's Liberation Army Unit (Eastern Region) occurred on the 9th October, 1980. This was known as 'Choro incident'. On the other hand it can also be regarded as a serious setback in the course of the armed revolutionary campaign of this organisation. The leaders also admitted that the lack of communication between the two groups was the responsible factor for this incident. It is said that the top leader of PLA, Shri N. Bisheshwor Singh with some senior leaders of the organisation were waiting for the arrival of another group which went to an area for a specific reason. The group was supposed to reach Choro within fifteen days. The purpose of the meeting was to discuss the future course of action and about the possible help which they were expecting to get from other foreign countries.[115] While they were coming towards Choro via Ashang Khullen at Tengnoupal area, they met a direct confrontation with Home Guards. Then they were dispersed in the thick jungle and some went towards Heirok and Pallel.[116] Thus this incident gave a temporary setback to the activities of PLA (Eastern Region). Choro is a tribal village situated in the border areas of the East District of Manipur. It is about 15 miles from Chassad village of the same district. It is said that the secret information about the establishment of their camp might be in the knowledge of the security personnel from the local sources. Whatever the case may be, after getting accurate information about the camping of PLA volunteers at this place, a combine force of Border Security Force (BSF) and Village Volunteer Force (VVF) marched towards the camp and raided in the afternoon of the 9th October, 1980. It is reported that in this raid, eight volunteers of PLA and one BSF jawan were killed[17] and the security personnel recovered eleven guns including one S.L.R. and three rifles. Then on the 15th October, in an official paper of the army, they claimed that Shri Bisheshwor was hit on his body due to the exchange of fire and the government also declared a reward of Rs. twenty-five thousand on his head.[118] Indeed, this incident was a very important turning point because after the clash. Shri N. Bisheshwor and his close associates came down to valley areas and established a new camp at Chingkhei Ching,[119] and training centres was opened at Baruni Chingkhong, Natum Ching and Keibi areas.[120] Thus with a new hope PLA again tried to intensify their activities. This revolutionary activities were regarded by some writers as 'burgeoning insurgency'.[121] It became a great concern to the government and to check their actions they also began to deploy army and other security personnel in sensitive places. In the meantime the state police arrested Shri Rajen Achouba Singh on the 11th December, 1980[122] from a hideout located at Bashikhong. Earlier, he was arrested by the police on the 11th November, 1978 from Kameng village but on 19th January, 1979 he escaped from the Medical College Hospital, Lamphel. His arrest was a very important breakthrough for the state government and a great loss for the organisation. However, PLA had continued their activities very effectively by adopting urban guerrilla type action mainly in the Imphal city. The action of the urban guerrilla revolution of PLA was clearly demonstrated on the 8th May, 1981. In the early morning of this day, a serious clash took place between the cadres of PLA and security personnel at Yaiskul Hiruhanba Leikai. The exchange of fire was continued for a quite long time and in this police operation two volunteers of PLA were killed and one person was arrested along with a granade.[123] The deceased persons were Shri Chongtham Somorjit Singh of Singjamei, son of an advocate, Ch. Nodiachand Singh and Th. Ibochouba Singh alias Bati of Yaiskul Chingakham Leirak, son of Late Ibohal Singh who was a sub-inspector of Police Department. Thus the People's Liberation Army Unit (Eastern Region) had successfully continued their armed campaign in various areas of Manipur and it created a serious law and order problem to the state government. On the other hand their ideological stand and objective has created a big problem to the Central government as they thought that the outbreak of separatist tendencies among the minds of the people was the work of other countries. The government also made a serious attempt to detract the moral and physical support of the common people to PLA by adopting various types of psychological propaganda warfare by issuing a number of pamphlates and distributing them to the people. By giving justification to the repressive measure of the authority, the Government of Manipur claimed that the army's operation was for the protection of life and property of 'loyal citizens'[124] and in the interest of the innocent public needs. They also said that the operation of army, which was claimed by PLA as 'an act of invasion by the Indian army', was a false propaganda and it was nothing but to deceive the people.[125] The Government had fixed the responsibility of the deteriorating law and order situation of the state to PLA. With these observations the government said that the army operation would be in Manipur till they finish their job.[126] Thus the revolutionary activities of PLA Unit (Eastern Region) became a serious concern to different sections of the people of Manipur. Regarding the nature of their activities it is observed that PLA was the most prominent underground group having a deep ideological concept of Mao's thought with secessionist aim. And from their method of operation it can be clearly seen that they had a very good foreign conctact.[127]

The 6th July, 1981 was a great red-letter day in the history of the revolutionary movement of People's Liberation Army Unit (Eastern Region). This day marked a turning point in the entire revolutionary process of this organisation and it was an unlucky day for the members of PLA. This particular incident is known in the later years as a 'Great Tekcham Incident'. This incident was equally important both for the Central and State Governments as well as of the organisation. For the government it was a major success on their ongoing process of repressive military action and for the revolutionary organisation it was a great setback. On this day the security personnel of the government killed some important hardcore PLA leaders and captured Shri N. Bisheshwor, the top leader of the organisation who was treated as an important revolutionary personality not only of the state but also of the entire region of North-East India. Tooshar Pandit, a journalist from outside Manipur regarded him as the 'legendary leader'[128] of the People's Liberation Army. He was arrested along with one Shashi Singh.

Teckcham is a village situated in the Thoubal District of Manipur. It is about 25 k.m. from Imphal. PLA made a remote area of this place as their makeshift hideout. It is said that they lived at this place for about two months just after the 'Choro incident'.[129] It was a mobile camp. They were planning to establish a camp in a secluded place but it was postponed due to the illness of their leader N. Bisheshwor. It is also reported that while they were in that area they could enjoy the moral and physical support of the villagers. So, with their support they were able to live in that area for a long time. In the mean time they also prepared to go out to another place and its preparation was also completed.[130] Unfortunately a day before the fateful day some of their men went out for some military action. One group was under the leadership of Raji Mangang and Joy and another was under Romeo alias Lemba,[131] and they were waiting for their return. So, on this particular day there were only nine members including N. Bisheshwor Singh. It is reported that after getting a quite positive information of the camping of underground people the Commanding Officer of 17 Jammu and Kashmir Rifles, Lt. Col. R.P. Sinha, prepared for an operation and a team was formed under the command of twenty-four year old 2nd Lt. Cyrus Phithawala who joined the army only about 22 months back.[131] Before taking a final decision for action Col. Sinha contacted Major General Nayar who was General Officer Commanding (GOC) of Manipur and Nagaland. After getting approval from GOC at about 2:30 in the afternoon, 2nd Lt. Pithawala with three J.C.Os and eighty other men left their camp for Tekcham.[133] From this fact it can be observed that the exact information about the presence of Bisheshwor was not in the knowledge of the army. Otherwise senior military officers would not give the responsibility of the operation to the junior officer. After moving for about 15 minutes from the main road the column was split into two. The column headed by 2nd Lt. Pithawala went straight for the hut, some 7 k.m. to the north where the PLA men were hiding. Another column moving further west took to the hill surrounding the village. At about 5.20 p.m. 2nd Lt. Pithawala and his men reached within 100 yards of the hut. It is said that on that day the PLA made a gross mistake on their part. Usually they always kept a strong vigil by putting a sentry on the top of the hillock to watch any possible movement of the army. But that day they did not posted any sentry.[134] It is mentioned that the sentry's duty of that day was assigned to Khogen but he was also exhausted due to the hard works in the camp. At the same time the members also thought that the security men had no notice of their movement. Ultimately this miscalculation brought the final tragedy of the organization.

The shooting started at around 5:30 p.m. The army claimed that the first shot came from the hut. Then the troops also started firing with their rifles within a range of 150 feet and 2nd Lt. Pithawala was hit by a bullet in his right shoulder. In the meantime Lt. Col. Sinha reached the spot with a support column of three officers and twenty men. He found that Pithawala was bleeding profusely but he refused to leave the firing spot. He wanted to see it to the end. Around 8 p.m., the sound of the exchange of fire stopped and the army reached at the door of the hut. Lt. Col. Sinha asked the inmate to surrender and promised that no harm will come to him. The inmate came out and asked Lt. Col. Sinha about his status in the army. The Colonel replied that he was an army, which was big enough for the inmate. The Colonel again asked him about the hiding place of Shri N. Bisheshwor Singh. The man slowly answered that he was Bisheshwor Singh.[136] It is said that Lt. Col. Sinha could hardly believe to see a person having a wide nose, disheveled hair and sagging eyes[137] and that too without carrying a gun while claiming himself as the leader of the militant insurgency. So, with great suspicious eyes he again asked him whether he was at Choro. The man replied that he was at Choro and from there he went to Asangkhullen and he stayed there for three days and he also mentioned the names of the persons with whom he stayed. His answer tallied with the information made Lt. Col. Sinha confirmed that the inmate was none other than Bisheshwor Singh, the top leader of the PLA.[138] Another volunteer of PLA was also arrested with Bisheshwor while he was trying to escape from the backside of the hut. He said that when the army reached the spot he was very busy as he was preparing dinner for other members.[139]

Thus with the arrest of Bisheshwor Singh the whole army action of 'Tekcham incident' came to an end. It is observed that "had it not been for PLA chief, there could have been more survivors as the underground members could not escape from the spot leaving behind their leader."[140] In this incident seven important hardcore members of this organisation sacrificed their lives for the sake of their leader. They were (1) Biramangol Singh alias Ibohal, (2) Indrajit alias Yaima, (3) Khogen alias Langlen, (4) Rajen Macha alias Koba (5) Khogen, (6) Inao, and (7) Shanti. It is said that 2nd Lt. Pthawala was severely injured by the bullet coming from the gun of Rajen Macha.[141] The army claimed that from this incident they had collected three automatic rifles, seven pistols, one carbine, and some ammunition, etc.[142] Taking the advantage of this new development, Rishang Keishing, the then Chief Minister of Manipur, in his appeal in July, 1981 asked the people to maintain peace so that all the energies could be directed towards the development and well-being of the people of Manipur.

As has been mentioned above the Tekcham incident was a major setback in the entire revolutionary activities of the People's Liberation Army Unit (Eastern Region). On the other hand, it marked the end of a revolutionary phase of PLA under the leadership of Bisheshwor and beginning of a new chapter of this organisation with a new approach and outlook under a new leadership. Whatever the case may be this phase of movement laid a basic ideological framework for a successful revolutionary movement in the future.

## PEOPLE'S REVOLUTIONARY PARTY OF KANGLEIPAK (PREPAK) (1977–1985):

The People's Revolutionary Party of Kangleipak, popularly known as PREPAK, was also another revolutionary organisation, which is still actively indulged in the armed movement for the establishment of a distinctive and separate political identity of Manipur outside the Indian Union. But the ongoing process of their activities may be broadly classified into two, i.e., from 1977 to 1985 and post 1985 period. The first period, from 1977 to 1985, was a very important phase of this revolutionary organisation. During this period the leaders of the People's Revolutionary Party of Kangleipak (PREPAK) laid a firm-rooted foundation with all the infrastructures including the ideology and principle, which is a pre-requisite of every armed revolutionary organisation. Like People's Liberation Army Unit (Eastern Region), PREPAK also gave a valuable contribution to the growth of the political and social consciousness on the issue of the establishment of a separate and distinctive identity of the people of Manipur, which they called it 'Kangleipak'.

The People's Revolutionary Party of Kangleipak was established as an armed revolutionary organisation in order to give freedom to those people who are not able to enjoy the above basic human rights in their respective countries.[143] On the basis of this objective and to establish a free country based on the principle of classless society, the People's Revolutionary Party of Kangleipak (PREPAK) was established on the 9th October, 1977 at the top of the Koubru hill. Another important objective of the organisation was to establish an independent Mongoloid society by giving defeat to the imperialist force that forcibly occupied Manipur on the 15th October, 1949.[144] On this day they also formed their armed wing known as 'Red Army' locally known as 'Phingang Lanmi'. On the other hand, the establishment of PREPAK as an armed underground organisation was the work of Young Universe Manipur (YUM) established on the 19th September, 1976 under the leadership of R.K. Tullachandra.[145] The main objective of the organisation was based on the principle of "Universal Peace and Understanding."[146] The first team of office bearers was led by R.K. Tullachandra as President. Then very soon, in collusion with some ex-R.G.M. men, the members of the organisation had adopted a decision to form a revolutionary party for the establishment of a separate political identity outside the Indian Union.[147]

The main objective of this organisation was to establish an independent and classless society (communism) in Manipur by crushing the class and neo-colonialism of Indian Government.[148] The PREPAK classified the class enemies in two different categories. The groups in the first category are: (a) Bourgeois Politicians, (b) Bureaucratic officers, (c) Big businessmen, (d) Contractor class and money lender class, (e) the thieves and criminals who played the role of spy of the enemy, and (f) ecclesiastical group. The groups in the second category are: (a) The big business group who comes from outside Manipur, and (b) imperialistic force of Indian government.[149] They called it imperialistic categories.

With regard to the bourgeois politician, the PREPAK alleged that this group of people were responsible for all these chaotic conditions faced by the common people. They said that this group is the main and severe enemy of the masses because, for the sake of their personal advantages, they surrendered the independence of Manipur to other people and still they are getting the respectability of the identity of the common people. PREPAK regarded these groups of people as the agents of the government for the harassment of the common people.

The PREPAK regarded the big 'bureaucratic officers' as the most corrupted, highly ambitious group who always helped the enemy in the process of the removal of the separate political and social identity of this people.

They also considered the 'big business groups' for their continuous attempt to take high profit from day-to-day essential commodities of the people. This class, according to the PREPAK, in collusion with the non-Manipuri businessmen, tried to suck the blood of the common people. So, they charged this class as a great enemy of the people.

The contractor and moneylender class were also condemned by PREPAK as the enemy of the people. They said that this group of people always forfeited the wages of the labourers and lend money on the system of mortgage by taking a big interest. So they tried to subdue the common and poor people so that they would not be able to rise again from the present economic position.

The PREPAK also said that the persons who indulged in robbery and crimes, were used by the enemy and rich people as their weapons. This group of people was used by the enemy in the process of the defeat of the independent movement of the revolutionist.

The people of 'ecclesiastical group' were also condemned by PREPAK for their dangerous role. They alleged that this group of people, in the name of religion, always tried to create a division among the people and they misguided the common people in the wrong path.[150]

The 'wealth drain' policy of the non-Manipuri big business class was highly condemned by PREPAK. They said that this group of people controlled all the means of production in their hand and sucked the blood of the local people.

PREPAK also said that the security personnel of the Government of India like, State Police, Central Police force, Para military force, big officers coming from outside Manipur, are the imperialist force of the Indian Government. These people rendered a good service to suppress the independent movement of the revolutionaries.[151] Thus, the People's Revolutionary Party of K ngleipak have given a clear picture about the class enemies in Manipur and their separate identity. Such type of a highly ideological explanation is the unique feature of this revolutionary organisation.

Apart from this the People's Revolutionary Party of Kangleipak (PREPAK) also placed a list of 13 points programme for the people of Manipur. They pledged that they would translate these programmes into action in order to establish a classless society based on the principle of economic equality.

First, PREPAK strongly asserted that the system of inequality in the possession of land would be abolished and the ownership of land would be given to the village or particular society. So long as a particular family was in the area of village, they should be governed by the practices of the village and would be the ownership of the land they possess. If they desired to leave the place, they had no authority to sell the land to any individual because land should be given back to the village or society.

Second, they also said that no individual or family could be the owner of a firm, industry, factory, etc. Everything should be in the name of the village or society or community. The labourers who are working in the factory shall be the owner of that factory.

Third, the state would act as the guardian of the children and all the possible and pre-requisite facilities of the education of the children would be provided by the State.

Fourth, PREPAK said that the vocational type of education would replace the present system of education. The children would be given a chance to attend the working system in the factory or industry. Certificate system would be abolished. This system, according to them, would provide job facilities to the children during the students' career.

Fifth, the training to the army would be in an entirely different system. PREPAK says that they would give training to the army not only on how to fight the external forces but also on how to deal with the danger from the 'fifth-columnist' in the society.

Sixth, all the organisations and newspapers, who always played a negative role against the revolutionary movement of the masses, would be abolished and a government by the workers and peasants (proletariats) would be established.

Seventh, in order to get the opportunity to express the desire of the people, the newspaper facilities would be established in every 'pana'.[152] Here the people would have the opportunity to give a critical observation against the government if they (government) committed mistakes.

Eight, the working style of Indian judicial system would be abolished and a new judicial system would be established in every 'Leikai', village and 'panas'.

Ninth, the present system of voting pattern would be abolished and the election of representatives of the community would be introduced with the system of the 'raised of hand' method among the voters.

Tenth, Lallup system[153] and collective workshop of the women would be introduced. Every citizen would be given military training. All the Leikais, villages would be the storehouse of the arm and ammunition and training centre.

Eleventh, a new method of agricultural system would be introduced in the pattern of industry. Women society would be equally respected according to their labour.

Twelve, the Indian bureaucratic working system and style of offices would be abolished and all the workers would be equally respected according to their labour.

Thirteenth, PREPAK would extend support to those people who suffered in the hands of imperialist force and internal colonialism. They would encourage the idea of revolutionary spirit in the world.[154]

These are the brief summary of points of programme placed by the People's Revolutionary Party of Kangleipak. From this fact it can be observed that the only objective of PREPAK was to establish a socialist society in Manipur after a successful armed revolution.

According to a report of 1977, the seven important leaders of the organisation namely (1) Tullachandra (Loyataba), (2) Ayekpam Dhiren Singh, (3) Kabikanta Sharma, (4) Ninghthoujam Imochouba, (5) Kritibabu Mangang, (6) Nandabir, and (7) Huidrom Tomba, took a pledge by touching the bullet of the gun by their teeth.[155] They made an open promise that being communists, they would respect the principle of Marxism and they will act for the welfare of the 'Meitei Society'[156] and country. The People's Revolutionary Party of Kangleipak also had an intention to enforce a strong and strict principle of the party among its members. They have given fifteen points principle or code of conduct of the party, which was to be followed by every members of the party. The code of conduct of the party strongly emphasized that every member of the party should be ready to accept the order of the party and the order and directive of the senior should be respected by the junior members. It is said that, to abide by the decision of the United Committee of the Party, would be the basic principle and duty of the party members. The principle of self-criticism was introduced in order to establish a healthy internal democratic system inside the party. The party also strongly emphasized to respect and honour the women community in the society and not to make any type of harassment to others. One of the most important duties which is to be performed very carefully by the cadres of the party was the secrecy of the working of the organisation. They strongly asserted that the members of the party should maintain the secrecy of the party even when they were arrested by the army. Finally, it is mentioned that if any member of the party had violated these code of conduct, the party would give severe punishment to them.[157]

Thus with these ideological framework and revolutionary principles, the People's Revolutionary Party of Kangleipak (PREPAK) also began to participate in the revolutionary movements in Manipur. The leaders of the party was also fully aware of the social, political and economic situation in Manipur and so they make a serious attempt to get the support of the common people by mixing with them in every social activities. At the same time they also tried to raise funds for the organisation. So, the first attempt of the leaders of the organisation was on two fronts i.e. to bring people on their side and to raise fund for the organisation. At this juncture the party faced a major jolt due to the untimely demise of two important leaders. It is mentioned that as part of the programme of the green revolution, PREPAK established a firm at Kameng on the western side of Imphal city and responsibilities was given to some members. Meanwhile the police got information about the suspicious movements of these youths. Therefore, on the 12th November, 1978 a combined force of Manipur police under the command of Shri Sunil Sharma, Sub-Inspector of Police and Shri Narendrapal, Commandant of CRPF attacked the firm of Kameng and killed Ayekpam Dhiren alias Angam and Shri Kabikanta Sharma alias Leingam the two prominent leaders of PREPAK. Along with them the security personnel also killed Gambhir Singh, a member of PLA. They arrested three persons. They were Shri Rajen Achouba, Radhakishore and Manaobi. The news of the murder of revolutionary youths spread like a wild fire and the people enmass gave a revolutionary salute to the departed soul of these youths.

In order to have a positive and effective revolutionary movement, both in action and ideology, the People's Revolutionary Party of Kangleipak also tried to establish a contact with the Chinese Government. In the year 1978, seven leaders of the Party, i.e., (1) R.K. Tullachandra Singh alias Loyataba, (2) Bonbihari, (3) Watham Krishnakanta alias Tayai, (4) Inaocha, (5) Ayekpam Surenmacha, (6) Imocha, and (7) Dillip went to Tibet to meet the Chinese leaders. They met Wang Swi, the Chairman of the local council of the Communist Party of China. The Chinese leaders advised them to launch a mass mobilization first and agreed to extend help later on. They even asked them to come back either within six or eight months. Accordingly an agreement of understanding was signed. But that agreement paper was lost at the demolition of Mapao Camp.[158] Just after the Kameng incident, another batch of four leaders i.e., (1) Watham Krishnachandra (Tayai), (2) Thambal, (3) Dillip, and (4) Shyamananda again went to Tibet but as they were not able to contact the right person they came back without getting any positive result.[156] Thus the PREPAK started their revolutionary activities very slowly and effectively. To see the revolutionary activities in the valley areas the Government of India, by an official notification declared the Peoples Revolutionary Party of Kangleipak as an 'outlawed organisation.'[159]

Then the Government of India, by an official notification declared a sum of Rs. 25,000 (Rupees twenty five thousand) on the head of R.K. Tullachandra alias Loyataba.[160] Thus the government also started to take repressive measures against the activities of the organisation. While this was the situation the police again arrested Shri R.K. Tullachandra Singh, the leader of the organisation on the midnight of 20th June, 1979 from the residence of a section officer at Khurai.[161] The arrest of R.K. Tullachandra was also another important major setback to the ongoing activities of the organisation. But this situation was quite temporary. In the late night of 2nd July, 1979 at about 11.00 p.m. Shri R.K. Tullachandra escaped from the custody of Singjamei Police Station along with a constable.[162] They also carried away one rifle with about 50 (fifty) ammunitions. It is reported that the name of the police constable was Shri Ibomcha Singh alias Leishabi. The escape of Tullachandra was a serious concern to the state government and on the other hand, it was also an eye opener to the government in regard to their weak points and lapses in the security arrangement.

Immediately the state government constituted a one-man enquiry committee to investigate the matter. Halim Chaudhury, the Deputy Commissioner of Central District was selected to enquire the matter.

After this the People's Revolutionary Party of Kangleipak (PREPAK) started a series of non-stop revolutionary activities in the state. They began to attack police outposts, which were stationed in different parts of Manipur particularly in valley areas. Their main objective was to collect the firearms from these police stations. The attack on the Moirang Police Station in one evening of September, 1979 was a major achievement of the volunteers of the party. In this incident the PREPAK activists killed one A.S.I. and two constables and took away 16 (sixteen) rifles. Apart from this they also adopted a revolutionary campaign against the prominent political personalities who were alleged by them as the enemies of the people of Manipur. They also condemned the merger of Manipur into India in 1949. They regarded it as an act of betrayal to the people of Manipur. Therefore they had adopted a stand to ask those political leaders who supported the merger to tender their apology to the people of Manipur. Even they prepared to give severe punishment to them. But it is mentioned that the stand of the party was not materialized due to the sudden attack on their camp by the police.[163] The raid by the police at the secret camp of Makhan at the foothill of Koubru hill on the 16th February, 1980 was a turning point in the history of the organisation. In this raid the police force completely destroyed the camp and it is also reported that they killed one Santikumar who was a sepoy in the Manipur Rifles. Then four days after this incident, i.e., on the 19th February, the security forces arrested five important persons of the organisation from the Mapao village at Sagolmang areas on the northern side of Imphal city. They were, (1) R.K. Tullachandra Singh, (2) Km. Sushila Devi, (3) Ibungomacha (4) Narendra, and (5) Ango, a tribal from Makhan village.[164] The arrest of R.K. Tullachandara Singh was a great achievement of the government. From there R.K. Tullachandra was kept in the custody of 4th Assam Rifles and then he was sent to jail. This was a tragic incident for the organisation because just after his arrest a serious problem of internal factionalism was developed inside the party. This issue created a serious confusion among the common people to know the real identity of the leadership of PREPAK.

A series of press notes and counter press notes were issued and pamphlets were distributed to the people on different versions. This created more confusion among the people to understand the identity of the party. In the meantime, R.K. Tullachandra made an appeal to his party members through All India Radio on the 20th February and 1st March, 1980[165] to give up the arm activities. In his radio message he strongly emphasized to adopt some kind of revolutionary approach without taking up the arms. He also appealed to his comrades to have their confidence in the developmental programme of Rajkumar Dorendro Singh, the Chief Minister of Manipur and his government. He also expressed his confidence in the integrity of the Chief Minister and said that through dialogue with the leadership of Indian Government Dorendro would bring some positive development for the welfare of the people.[166] In a cyclostyle pamphlet issued by Propaganda Committee of PREPAK the party expressed their reservation to the appeal of R.K. Tullachandra.[167] On the other hand the party, by observing all the prevailing situations, asked the people to analyze his speech very carefully. Again in a press note issued on 17th March, 1980 by Propaganda Committee, the party categorically stated that they would not give up arm until they achieved their goal.[168] The press note also accused five leaders of the Party namely, (1) R.K. Tullachandra, (2) Ibobi Singh, (3) Sushila, (4) Ibochouba, and (5) Tayai. The pamphlet also alleged that these five people gave order to kill Shri Th. Bira Singh, a leader of Communist Party of India and they, in collusion with the government, tried to abolish the revolutionary activities of PREPAK.[169] Again in a press note, issued by the Propaganda Committee, the thirteen leaders of the organisation were declared as the counter group. The decision was taken by the Central Committee meeting held on 19th and 20th March.[170] On the other hand, the other group charged Shri Maipak Sharma, the leader of another faction, of taking a sum of Rs. 1.40 lakh (Rupees one lakh forty thousand) only from the government.[171] At the same time the other group had declared a reward of Rs. 10,000 (Ten thousand) on the head of ten leaders. It is mentioned that they would give this money to those persons who was able to arrest them.[172] The names were, (1) Krishnachandra alias Tayai, (2) Imochouba, (3) Suren Macha, (4) Suren Achouba, (5) Dillip, (6) Kritibabu, (7) Gitchandra, (8) R.K. Dollen, (9) Medha, (10) Shanti, etc. Thus a series of internal clashes was going on inside the organisation of People's Revolutionary Party of Kangleipak. One group was led by one Maipak Sharma who was once a member of 'Black Nationalist' Organisation.[173] The other members who came with Maipak Sharma was Som Sharma, Radhakishore Sharma, etc. The other group was still led by R.K. Tullachandra. This internal conflict became very serious and it was continued for quite long time. During this period of conflict many important leaders of the party became the victims. The killing of R.K. Chitrasen, the younger brother of R.K. Tullachandra and Keisham Ibobi on the 16th March, 1980 at Ayangpalli was the most important and notable example of the conflict of factionalism. The exchange of fire between the two factions on the 31st March, 1980 at Ayangpalli was the most important example of the conflict. In the meantime, the PREPAK of R.K. Tullachandra also continued revolutionary activities by attacking the security persons and police outposts at different places in the valley area. The killing of three CRPF personnel at Langjing on 26th April, 1980 was a major operation of PREPAK. In retaliation of their action the CRPF personnel killed four innocent people. As a mark of protest against the killing of innocent people all the womenfolk of Manipur came out openly and launched a big women's movement against the security people of Indian Government. Thus the involvement of women against the Indian army was indeed a great achievement of PREPAK. The urban guerilla warfare tactics of PREPAK was a big concern to the state government and the centre. Therefore the government adopted different types of methods to stop the revolutionary activities of the organisation. In the way of their activities, fifteen volunteers of PREPAK surrendered to the Chief Minister.[174]

Apart from their armed activities, the leaders of the PREPAK also make a serious attempt to establish good relationship and coordination with the other revolutionary organizations of different states of North East Region. It is reported that the party was able to establish relation with Mizo National Front (MNF) in the year 1980. They also established contact with Tripura National Volunteer (TNV), a revolutionary organisation in Tripura. In addition to this they also tried to establish relationship with National Socialist Council of Nagaland (NSCN).[175] Thus the leaders of PREPAK made a large-scale attempt to launch a massive revolutionary activities with the co-operation and understanding with the revolutionary organizations of the state and North Eastern Region.

The year 1985 was very important for the People's Revolutionary Party of Kangleipak. As was stated above due to the constant and continuous internal factionalism the organisation was not able to carry the masses with them. On the other hand, the repeated change of leadership created some kind of instability in the organizational matter of the party. In that year R.K. Tullachandra Singh was released from the jail. He gain joined the party and began to work for the consolidation and strengthening of the position of the organisation. It is mentioned that for about one month, nine leaders of the party, namely, R.K. Tullachandra, Soraisam Wanglen, Thockchom Shamo, Dillip, Rajkumar Khomdon, Jilla, Urikkhinbam Madanmacha, Khelemba and Khuraijam Sanatombi encamped at the top of the Laimatol hill of Laimaram[176] and there they decided to do some armed action with an objective to show the existence of the party. Accordingly, on the 12th November, 1985 at about 4.30 p.m., they attacked the post of 7th Manipur Rifles at Kabowakching. They gave a very good fight and later the sepoys of the 7th Manipur Rifles got the upper hand and killed R.K. Tullachandra at the spot and other members escaped.

Thus, the untimely death of R.K. Tullachandra alias Loyataba was a turning point in the history of the revolutionary activities of People's Revolutionary Party of Kangleipak. It marked the end of a phase of the PREPAK under the leadership of R.K. Tullachandra and beginning of another organizational set-up under a new leadership. Therefore, the 12th November, 1985 closed the chapter of the contribution of PREPAK under the leadership of R.K. Tullachandra.

## KANGLEIPAK COMMUNIST PARTY (KCP) (1979/1980-1995):

The Kangleipak Communist Party (KCP) was also another important revolutionary organisation which operates mainly in the valley areas of Manipur. Like other armed revolutionary organizations, they also launched the armed movement with an objective to establish a separate political identity of the people of Manipur outside the political jurisdiction of Indian Union. According to an official pamphlet of the party, the Kangleipak Communist Party was established in the year 1980 after having a meeting of all the different cadres of the party for two days, i.e., May 14th and 15th, 1980.[177] But according to Konjengbam Binoy Singh, an ex-leader of KCP, the party was established on the 28th April, 1980 at Thembou village, situated at the hill in Kangpokpi area by some members.[178] On other hand, according to an official report, i.e., 'A Report on Special Convention of Kangleipak Communist Party, August 13th, 1994' the organisation was established on 20th August, 1979 at Mapao Village.[179] It is also recorded that the Kangleipak Communist Party was established under the leadership of Yendrembam Ibohanbi alias Baji on the 14th April, 1980.[180] Therefore, it is not very clear about the actual date of the establishment of the Kangleipak Communist Party as an armed revolutionary organisation in Manipur. The most important point which can be noted down in this respect is the different version in the official papers of the party. It creates more confusion and obscurity in the fixation of the date and year of the establishment of the party.

The basic objective of the party was to establish an independent Manipur which they called 'Kangleipak' by removing all the political parties, all the political agents, Indian imperialist force which was regarded by them as the greatest enemy of the people. Their motto was to have a sovereign independent Manipur based on national cause and national politics.[181] They claimed that Kangleipak Communist Party stands for the people of Manipur (Kangleipak), for the entire people of the North-Eastern Region of India, for the people of the South East Asia and for the workers and peasants and for those persons who strongly desire to establish independent state based on classless society.[182] They also made an appeal to all the revolutionary organizations in the state to stop all kinds of internal conflicts and clashes, which was going on among themselves and asked them to join together under the roof of an umbrella for the complete removal of their common enemy. In regard to the social and cultural policies the KCP had categorically asserted that they would pay respect to all types of religious beliefs and culture which were enjoyed by the people of the different ethnic groups in Manipur. They also strongly emphasized that they would give proper attention and protection to the practices of different cultures and traditions of the people of hill areas of this place including the Muslim community. Under these social and cultural policies. they would encourage the people of Manipur (Kangleipak) to live together in a most harmonious way of life.

With these political and cultural policies the Kangleipak Communist Party began to launch their armed revolutionary activities in Manipur. Indeed, the birth of KCP as a revolutionary organisation was also a great significant development in the history of the revolutionary movement in Manipur. At the beginning their area of operation was confined only in the eastern side of the Imphal valley. The areas which were used by the KCP as operational areas were also the nerve centre of the armed movement of Hijam Irabot Singh in the year 1948-1951. So to launch an armed struggle with the active participation of the people of highly revolutionary spirit have produced a new impact in the minds of the other people of the state. But unfortunately the KCP was also not free from the internal crisis. As a result of this they were not able to move forward in order to implement their objective very successfully. This development was a great advantageous situation to the security personnels of the government. Except for some sporadic armed activities, the organisation was not able to expand their ideological principle and objective to the masses in a large scale way. On the other hand the suppressive measures adopted by the government of the state also formed an important contributing factor for the slow pace of the armed movement of KCP. During the course of their armed struggle they had the experience of many ups and downs. One of the biggest setbacks of the organisation was the capture of Ibohanbi, the Commander-in-Chief of the Red Army, along with four activists from Sekta. According to the press note of the 'Defence Wing' of the government, the arrest of Ibohanbi, the Commander-in-Chief of KCP, was a great breakthrough to the policy of the suppressive measure of the government. They also claimed that their arrest would be a great opportunity for the government to remove the whole armed activities and organisation work of the party once for all.[183] The organisation had also suffered mainly from the betrayal of some party members. This was clearly mentioned in their official report.[184] Thus for quite long time the party faced a serious internal factional crisis. But in spite of all these problems the existence of the party was successfully reached to the knowledge of the common people of Manipur. The party leaders and activists who strongly convinced to the cause and ideology always made a successful attempt to move forward to the path of victory. While this situation was going on, the party again faced a serious jolt. It was on the 1st July, 1995 that an exchange of fire took place between KCP and CRPF at Heituppokpi at Andro near Nongmaiching Hill (Baruni Hill). In this encounter the CRPF personnels killed the founder leader Yendrembam Ibohanbi. The untimely death of Ibohandbi was, indeed, a great setback in the whole revolutionary process of KCP. On the other hand it also brought a new chapter in the revolutionary activities under the leadership of Ibohanbi and opening of a new chapter of activities without his leadership. This day is regarded by KCP as an important day for the organisation and still they remember it as a 'Black Day'.[185] Thus with the death of Ibohanbi an important phase of revolutionary activities of the organisation was over and it marked the beginning of a new phase under a different leadership.

## NOTES

1. Administrative Report of Manipur, 1967-68.
2. Contantine, R. 1981. *Manipur: Maid of the Mountains*. P. 89.
3. Ibid.
4. *Prajatantra* (A Manipuri local daily). 25.01.1996.
5. *Huyen Lanpao* (A Manipuri local daily). 14.9.1994.
6. Wangkheirakpam Tomba Singh of Keibi village was the informant of the writer.
7. Ibid.
8. Nileh was the nephew of Mr. Daiho, a political leader of Manipur (W.Tomba Singh was the informant of the writer).
9. W. Tomba Singh was the informant of the writer.
10. Ibid.
11. Sarangthem Mani Singh, was the informant of the writer.
12. W. Tomba Singh was the informant of the writer.
13. Ibid.
14. Ibid.
15. Constantine, R. Op.cit.P.90.
16. *Administrative Report of Manipur 1972-73*. P.4.
17. Constantine, R. Op.cit. P.90.

18. Statement of the Central Committee of the United National Liberation Front issued on 24th November, 1992 on the occasion of the 28th Anniversary. P.3.
19. Ibid.
20. Ibid.
21. Ibid.
22. 'United National Liberation Front na Miyamda Sengdokchaba' (A clarification to the people by UNLF). A pamphlet issued on 12.05.1992. P.5.
23. Sanasam Mangi Singh of Mongsangei was the informant of the writer.
24. File No.8/6(3)/79 D.I.G., C.I.D., Government of Manipur.
25. Ibid.
26. Tarapot Phanjoubam. 1993. *Insurgency Movement in North East India.* P.43.
27. N. Bisheshwor Singh was the informant of the writer.
28. S. Mangi Singh was the informant of the writer.
29. Tarapot Phanjoubam. Op.cit. P.43.
30. Constantine, R. Op.cit. P.107.
31. Ibid.
32. Confessional statement of A. Khomdon Singh on 27.8.1969.
33. Tarapot Phanjoubam. Op.cit. P.4.
34. Ibid. P.41.
35. Ibid.
36. Confessional statement of H. Khomdon Singh on 27.8.1969.
37. Criminal Miscellaneous Petition. Op.cit. P.4.
38. Ibid.
39. Tarapot Phanjoubam. Op.cit.p.43.
40. Criminal Miscellaneous Petition. Op.cit. P.4.
41. Ibid. Pp.7-8.
42. Ibid. Pp.9.
43. Ibid. Pp.10.
44. *Prajatantra.* 16.5.1969.
45. Confessional statement of Mr. Ibohal Singh at the presence of R.N Chakravarty, S.D.M. on.27.08.1969.
46. *Prajatantra.* 19.02.1969.
47. Confessional statement of Shri Phurailatpam Toto Sharma

48. Constantine, R. Op.cit. P.110.
49. N. Bisheshwor Singh was the informant of the writer.
50. *Prajatantra*. 24.11.1969.
51. Ibid.
52. Ibid.
53. Ibid.
54. Letters from the 23 R.G.M. volunteers in the jail to the Lt. Governor of Manipur.
55. *Administrative Report 1972-73*. Government of Manipur. P.4.
56. *Dawn*. Vol. III. 1980. (Published by PLA). P.22.
57. Contantine, R. Op.cit. P.113.
58. N. Bisheshwor was the informant of the writer.
59. *Dawn*. Vol. II. 1979. (Pub. by PLA). P.22.
60. Ibid. P.22.
61. Soram Hemba was the informant of the writer.
62. File No.8/6(3)/79-SP (CID) Secret Police Dept., Government of Manipur.
63. Ibid.
64. Ibid.
65. Bisheshwor Singh was the informant of the writer.
66. S. Henba Singh was the informant of the writer.
67. Chirom Ranjit Singh's speech in the seminar on Insurgency on the 9th September, 1989, organised by the Committee of Concerned Citizens at State Guest House.
68. N. Bisheshwor was the informant of the writer.
69. *Dawn*. Vol. III. 1979. P.30.
70. Ibid. Pp.30-31.
71. Ibid. P.30.
72. N. Bisheshwor was the informant of the writer.
73. File No.8/6(3)/79 DIG (CID), Government of Manipur.
74. N. Bisheshwor was the informant of the writer.
75. Speech of Chirom Ranjit on 9th September, 1989.
76. Ibid.
77. Ibid.
78. N. Bisheshwor Singh was the informant of the writer.
79. Speech of Chirom Ranjit. Op.cit.
80. N. Bisheshwor Singh was the informant of the writer.

81. Ibid.
82. *Dawn*.Vol. II. 1979. P.8.
83. Ibid. P.9.
84. Ibid
85. Ibid.
86. Ibid. P.23.
87. *Dawn*. Vol. I. 1979. P.12.
88. Ibid. P.13.
89. Ibid. P.2.
90. *Dawn*. Vol. I. 1979. P.3.
91. *Dawn*. Vol. II. 1979. P.11.
92. Ibid.
93. Ibid. P.12
94. *Indian Express*. (An English national daily). September 30, 1980.
95. 'P.L.A. na miyamda laothokchaba' (A declaration of P.L.A. to the people). A pamphlet issued by the P.L.A.
96. Ibid.
97. Ibid.
98. *Dawn*. Vol. II. 1979. P.20.
99. Ibid. P.22.
100. Ibid. P.20.
101. Ibid. P.22.
102. Ibid. P.23.
103. *Porumlen Apunba*. Vol. 5. Written and published by N. Bisheshwor. Quoted in *Kangleipak Revolution* by P. Labango Singh. 1997. P.71.
104. *Dawn*. Vol. II. 1979. P.21.
105. *Dawn*. Vol. I. 1979. P.22.
106. 'P.L.A. Na Miyamda Laothokchaba' (A declaration of P.L.A. to the people). A pamphlet issued by the P.L.A. P.11.
107. *Indian Express*, 30.09.1979.
108. 'P.L.A. Na Miyamda Laothokchaba' (A declaration of P.L.A. to the people). A pamphlet issued by the P.L.A. P.11.
109. Pamphlet issued by P.L.A. on 26.04.1979.
110. *Prajatantra* (A local Manipuri daily newspaper). 6.5.1979.
111. Ibid.

112. An Announcement of cash reward for information leading to the capture of Meitei Extremists, a leaflet issued by the Government of Manipur.
113. *Prajatantra*. 11.5.1979.
114. *Dawn*.
115. Tarapot. Op.cit. P.60.
116. Ibid.
117. *Prajatantra*. 11.10.1980.
118. Ibid.
119. Tarapot. Op.cit. P.73.
120. Ibid.
121. Ibid.
122. *Prajatantra*. 14.12.1980.
123. *Khollao* (A local Manipuri daily newspaper). 09.05.1981.
124. 'PLA Misguides Youth' (A pamphlet issued and distributed by the Government of Manipur).
125. Ibid.
126. Ibid.
127. *Amrita Bazar Patrika* (A daily English paper). 01.05.1981.
128. *Sunday* (A weekly English Magazine published by Anand Bazar publication). Calcutta. 9-15 May, 1982.
129. Shashi Singh, an ex-member of P.L.A. was the informant of the writer.
130. Ibid.
131. Ibid.
132. *Sunday*. Op.cit. P.9.
133. Ibid.
134. Shashi was the informant of the writer.
135. Tarapot. Op.cit. P.94.
136. *Sunday*. Op.cit. P.9.
137. Ibid.
138. Ibid.
139. Shashi was the informant of the writer.
140. Tarapot. Op.cit. P.99.
141. Labango, P. Op.cit. P.75.
142. *Paojel* (A local Manipuri Newspaper). 08.07.1981.
143. A pamphlet issued by the Information and Publicity Department, PREPAK on the 16th anniversary of the organisation. P.1.

144. Ibid.
145. Labango. P. Op.cit. P.87.
146. Ibid. P.88.
147. Manifesto of People's Revolutionary Party of Kangleipak. P.1
148. Ibid. Pp.1-8.
149. Ibid.Pp. 10-11.
150. Ibid. Pp.1-12.
151. Ibid.
152. In the early period, the Meiteis were divided into four groups, viz., Leipham, Khaba, Ahallup and Naharup. Each groups is known as a 'pana'.
153. It is a system introduced by the king of Manipur from the early period. Under this system every able person between the age of 17 and 60 years have to attend the royal service for 10 days out of 40 days. This system was known as 'lallup' system.
154. Manifesto of PREPAK. Pp.13-18.
155. Labango, P. Op.cit. Pp.88.
156. Ibid. P.89.
157. Manifesto of PREPAK. Op.cit. Pp.20-21.
158. Ibid. P.91.
159. *Prajatantra*. 28.10.1979.
160. Ibid. 06.05.1979.
161. Ibid. 21.06.1979.
162. Ibid. 04.07.1979.
163. Labango, P. Op.cit. P.92.
164. *Prajatantra*. 22.02.1980.
165. Labango, P. Op.cit. P.93.
166. Text of the radio speech of Tullachandra reproduced in *Prajatantra* daily on 07.03.1980.
167. *Prajatantra*. 12.3.1980.
168. Ibid.20.03.1980.
169. Ibid. 20.03.1980.
170. Ibid. 26.03.1980.
171. Ibid. 27.03.1980.
172. Ibid.27.03.1980.
173. Labango, P. Op.cit. P.90

174. *Prajatantra*. 22.09.1980.
175. Labango. P. Op.cit. P.98
176. Ibid. P.99.
177. Kangleipak Communist Party (KCP). A Pamphlet issued by the National Polictical Advisory Red Army signed by N. Babu Meitei. In-charge Chairman.
178. *Lanmei Thanbi*. October. 1985. Vol. III. No.6. P.15.
179. Labango, P. Op.cit. P.111.
180. *Anouba*. December. 1996. P.53. Quoted in P. Labango. Op.cit. P.111.
181. Kangleipak Communist Party. Pamphlet. Op.cit.
182. Ibid.
183. *Huyen Lanpao*. 27.05.1981.
184. A Report on Special Convention of Kangleipak Communist Party. August 13.1994. Quoted in P. Labango. Op.cit.
185. Labango, P. Op.cit. P.114.

# CHAPTER FOUR

# LEADERSHIP

A person who is occupying a central role or position of dominance and influence in a group is commonly known as "Leader". The position and function of the leader is known as 'Leadership'. According to K.D. Ganagrade, leadership is a group process through which individuals initiate activities for delivering the common objectives of the community by working together, stimulating each other, supplementing abilities and resources, and evolving an effective organizational or hierarchical pattern.[1] This concept of 'Leadership' is said to have been derived from the leadership in a religious sectarian setting or in group of primary relationship.[2] It is further mentioned that 'the solitary, dramatic personality who mobilized and inspired masses to new goals and methods of religious salvation became an important prototype of leadership'.[3] The existence of leadership is universally accepted as a natural human phenomenon in every society. It is a known fact that society is a body of individuals living as members of a community or human being collectively associated or viewed as members of the community. In such collective group the members naturally requires a leader to lead in coordinating, controlling, directing or mobilizing the efforts of others in establishing the purposes, goals or objectives of the group. From the perspective of sociology many writers are of the view that leadership is the exercise of power or influence in social collectivities, such as groups, organizations, communities or nation. It is true that in society the leadership has to play many roles. Their primary role was to co-ordinate, control, direct, guide or mobilize the efforts of others. A leader may be engaged in a number of activities like maintaining the integrity and viability of the collectivity against internal and external threats and to play a vital role in motivating members to accept the collective goals. On the other hand, it is also a fact that the role of the leadership in any given society may not be a permanent feature. Their act of leading may be of very brief duration but the concept of leader implies a role relationship of some duration. From this angle it can be suggested that a leader is one who is repeatedly perceived to perform acts of leading. In the same line some writers said that the leader's position is occupied for a considerable time by the same individual. In this regard Pigors wrote. "leadership is a concept applied to the personality environment relation to describe the situation when a personality is placed in the environment that his 'will' feeling and insight direct and control others in the pursuit of a common cause."[6]

It is very clear that the role of the leader is to co-ordinate the members of the collective individuals and to guide in the proper direction. So, when the concept of leadership is being discussed the idea of followers is to be followed in the process of the discussion. There can be no leader without following and vice versa. In one sense the followers mean the persons in the group. There, the concept of group is also equally important when the role of leadership is to be discussed. Group means two or more individuals interacting in the pursuit of common and compatible goals. So, the duty of the leadership is to fulfill the issue of the group. Indeed, the idea of leadership occurs only within the group. In one way the leader and followers or group are collaborators. It is said that the leadership status itself is within a group and not outside of it. From this basic common understanding it can also be suggested that the idea of leadership emerges only when there is a necessity in the interest of the group. The natural process for the emergence of the leadership occurs when an individual member or some members start to take more active role within the group than others with a view to be preferred by others, to be listened to with more respect than others and to be dominant over others. The opportunity to be the leader of the group is always given by the situation which may directly and indirectly affect the interest of the members of the group. In such situation, the members of the group have given the opportunity to these individuals or particular member who possessed the characteristics of bravery, knowledge, skill and self-confidence, to be emerged as leaders. Stogdill rightly pointed out that "a person does not become a leader solely by virtue of any particular pattern of personality traits but rather by possession of any attributes that, by virtue of its relevance to the situation and its situationally determined evaluation by other group members, establishes a relationship of leading-following".[7] Thus, the groups, when the crisis situation occurs, have selected leader who can diagnose problems quickly and decisively. On the other hand the role of the leadership varies with situations because it is a nexus of need fulfillment that binds situational demand and group membership. From this fact it can be said that the leadership is a function of acceptance by followers. Unless the members of the group or followers accept the representation of the leadership he cannot be called a leader. It is also true that all kinds of leadership take place through the communication of ideas to the mind of others and if the presented ideas are not congenial to the minds of members, they will be rejected. In fact leadership is a status of the working relationship among the members of group in which the leader acquired through their active participation commitment and positive demonstration.

Lester G. Seligman also makes an attempt to analyze the idea of leadership from the modern political aspect. He said, "Leadership is a solution to the problems of both excessive and insufficient political power. Strong executive leadership was offered as a solution to two general and characteristic maledier of political system."[8] In his first observation he was of the view that the breakdown of traditional norm fostering groups leaves society open to conflict. In such situation a strong leadership is required as a substitute for 'cetrophied traditional primary group identifications - community, church, family, etc.'[9] He was of the view that such situation could be overcome and avoided by strong political leadership. He further mentioned that a strong and effective leader would be able to give integrative direction and action as a cure for the "stalemated pluralism endemic"[10] particularly to the western democracy. According to him only strong executive leader would furnish decisive national purpose when the society is not able to make in the right direction. Indeed the leader is to play two integrated functions; one, as a national hero and another, as political broker or outfit synthesizer. Actually these two roles, though it has got its own distinctive characters, cannot live separately. For example, when the idea of national consensus becomes a problematic, the 'broker' comes to power when a viable consensus exists. Sometimes, to some extent, the chief executive had to play both roles.

Some writers particularly the political scientists, and sociologists categorized the leadership into three different types, viz., Authoritarian leadership, Democratic leadership and Laissez-faire leadership.

(i) Authoritarian leadership: It is a form of leadership under which the leader or body of leaders always decides the goals and rules of the behaviour of a group. All the policies and directives were determined by the leader, and the dictated task would be carried on by the co-workers. It is said that under this system of leadership, the leader personally praises and criticizes each member, but remain aloof from active group participation.

(ii) Democratic leadership: It is a form of leadership in which the leader or body of leaders believes in and acts in accordance with a social role that supports certain democratic attitude, beliefs and values.[11] Under this system all the policy matters and decisions are finalized through the active participation of members in the decision making process along with the active participation of the leader. It is also mentioned that the democratic leader is 'objective' in his approach and criticism and tries to be group member in spirit without doing too much of the work.[13]

(iii) Laisser-faire leadership: Under this form of leadership the policy and decision would be finalized by the individual members of the group with minimum participation of the leader. It is said that the leader would provide materials and information when he was asked to do so but he would neither praise nor criticize group members.

Again some sociologists make an attempt to categorize three different forms of leadership authority viz., Charismatic leadership, Traditional leadership and Legal leadership. 'Charismatic leadership' leads the group or community by virtue of the extra ordinary powers attributed to them by their followers. Under 'Traditional leadership' the person or persons leads by virtue of custom and practice. Such leadership is possible only in a family or small community. The 'Legal leadership' is based on expertise and implemented according to formal rules. It is said that this type of leadership is formed in public administration and modern business enterprises.[14]

Indeed, the role of the leadership is the most important factor of any type of social movements, particularly in the case of the revolutionary movements, the role of the leadership is the 'predominant' factor for the success and failure of the ongoing revolutionary process. As mentioned in the previous chapter revolution is the politics of rapid and violent social change. In such condition the leaders always play a vital role for the success of the revolution. In regard to the real character of a revolutionary leader, E. Victor Wolfenstein observed that "the revolutionary leader is a man who exercises power and authority with respect to somebody of followers in terms of a revolutionary ideology". From this fact it is quite clear that the success and failure of any type of revolutionary movement lies on the sincerity, honesty, integrity, wisdom and accommodative nature of the leader. It is also suggested that there are two types of leadership in a revolutionary movement, i.e., vocational and avocational revolutionist. A leader who always devotes all his energies and times to the goals of the organisation of which he is a member and who is exposed to the ideology of his organisation may be treated as a revolutionary of 'vocation' type and a revolutionary leader whose activity is only an occasional one and his reason for participation is always secondary may be treated a revolutionary leader of 'avocation' type.

As a whole, leadership plays a vital role for the success of any type of revolution. There are a lot of evidences about the failure of the revolutionary movement in the world. Many factors were responsible for failures. Among them the role of the leadership is one of the most indispensable reason. Indeed, a revolutionary leader must have the capabilities to see the possible outcome of the process of the movement which are likely to be faced by the masses of the society. So, one of his or their responsibilities is to lay a firm foundation in order to meet any type of eventuality. As already mentioned above about the degree of importance of a leader, a revolutionary leader should emerge from a particular group of the society who sacrifices his mind and spirit to the cause of the revolution. The idea of confusion in his approach, the misunderstanding among the members of the society should be cleared first before the revolutionary idea is translated into action. This is also another basic duty of the revolutionary leadership. In short it can be suggested that if a revolutionary movement is launched by a leader or a group of leaders who are not very clear about the basic line of the approach or who are guided by the highly temporary emotional idea it will give a serious effect not only to the society of the present generation but it will also lead to the complete destruction of the path of the people of the next generation. If this trend comes to society definitely it would be the last stage of the existence of the separate identity of the people of the society. The lack of the will and ability of the leader to persevere in a revolutionary cause of action after the first demonstration or fighting had taken place[15] i the most crucial point for the failure of the revolutionary movement. The reason was that they feared anarchy and radicalism in their own ranks more than they feared their enemies.[16] Whatever the case may be the most important aspect for the success of a revolution lies in the personalities of the leader.

## THE MEITEI STATE COMMITTEE (MSC)

As stated above the 'Meitei State Committee' was established as an armed revolutionary organisation with an objective to make Manipur an independent country. The idea of the formation of this organisation was mooted by some youths who were actively involved in the armed struggle of 1948-1951 led by Hijam Irabot Singh. It is a well-known fact that the armed revolutionary movement of H. Irabot Singh was to establish a sovereign independent Manipur based on the socialistic pattern of society. So, the principle of classless society and idea of independent Manipur was very much in their mind. At the same time a strong sense of nationalism and patriotism was also very much involved in their approach. So, when they have come across a very good experience of the working style and the revolutionary spirit of the 'Naga Underground Movement' they took it as a great favourable time of the people of Manipur to strike for the achievement of their long standing aspiration of the idea of independent state. From this historical fact it can be observed that the idea of establishment of 'Meitei State Committee' as a revolutionary organisation was the decision of the collective leadership. It was not the work of the initiative of any individual leadership. Then later on those members who took initiative for the formation of this organisation offered leadership to Shri Wangkheirakpam Tomba Singh of Keibi Village, who was also another important participant and an active member of the armed revolutionary movement of Irabot Singh.

The detail information about the family background of Wangkheirakpam Tomba Singh was not very clear. However it is true that he was born and brought up in a peasant family. Perhaps due to his surrounding environmental situation, he did not have a vast knowledge of modern education. But at least he can read and write Manipuri. Over and above he had an intensive knowledge about political, economic and social conditions of Manipur. Before he went to underground he was a member of 'District Organizing committee' (D.O.C.) which was perhaps a branch of Communist Party of India, Assam Unit. For quite long time, particularly during the underground period, he was closely associated with Hijam Irabot Singh. Then after the formal establishment of the Communist Party of India, Manipur Unit he became a member of the party. But he left the party as soon as his request to provide ticket to him for contesting assembly election was not accepted by the party. At this juncture some youths asked him to take the responsibility of leadership of this revolutionary movement. After accepting their request Shri Tomba Singh took the leadership and gave a commendable services for the growth and strengthening of the party. Indeed, he performed his duty very successfully as a responsible leader of a revolutionary organisation. Another noteworthy quality of Shri Tomba Singh was that he never surrendered himself to the security people and authority of the state government. When the majority of the members of his organisation surrendered to the state government he refused to submit to the government and so he was arrested and put him inside the jail for two years. He even refused to take money under the scheme of the rehabilitation programme of the government.

Sarangthem Mani Singh of Waikhong Village was also another founder member and an important leader of the Meitei State Committee. He was the son of S. Amuba Singh, a farmer by profession. He was an illiterate person. But his commitment to the ideology and principle of the party compelled him to become an important member of the Communist Party of India and a follower of Hijam Irabot Singh. But he did not participate in the underground activities of the movement of 1948-51. However, in his best limited knowledge he was a staunch believer in the ideology of Marxism and at the same time he was also very much in favour of the establishment of a distinctive and separate political identity of Manipur, based on the principle of classless society, of socialism. Apart from this, like his late leader he also thought that a successful armed movement for a separate political identity could be possible only when there is a unity between hill and plain people. So when the news of the Naga Underground Movement came out to the knowledge of the public he thought that if the people of the valley area had joined hands with them it could be a meaningful movement for the whole people of the region. He also said that actually he was not in favour of the nomenclature "Meitei State Committee". But since their proposed name of "Manipur State Committee" was not acceptable to the leaders of the Naga Underground Movement they were compelled to review it again. As stated in the proceeding chapter the Naga underground leaders claimed that as they had already began to fight for the independence of Naga inhabited areas, the question of covering the whole area of Manipur was not advisable. So, they insisted to form only for the valley area. Accordingly he proposed the nomenclature of "Meitei State Committee"[17] as a name of their organisation. Under the repressive measure of the security forces of the State Government he was arrested from his house while he was preparing to go to the field and put him in jail for six months. Then he was released from jail and he received a sum of Rs. 2000 (Two thousand) from the government under the rehabilitation programme.

Another important leader of the organisation was Rengdol. He was a young man of Kom community of Utonglok near Leitanpokpi.[18] His background was not clearly known. But he was also a strong believer in the idea of the unity between the people of valley and hill areas. On the basis of this principle he joined the Meitei State Committee and took an active part by taking the responsibilities of the militant wing of the organisation. At that time the militant wing was put under joined command of three persons. They were (1) Hourungbam Angou Singh of Lousangkhong, (2) Rengdol, and (3) Soibam Yaima Singh of Patlou. It is said that the agents of the State Government repeatedly asked Shri Rengdol to surrender and they also promised him to provide all required facilities for his future life. It seems that Shri Rengdol was convinced by the assurances of the Government and accordingly he surrendered to the State authorities and in return to this he received Rs. 2000 (Two Thousand) under the rehabilitation programme of the Government of Manipur.[19]

Other important leaders of this organisation were Angom Ibohal Singh of Patlou village, Oinam Tombi Singh of Keibi Heikak Mapan, Hourungbam Angou Singh of Keibi who was claimed as the deputy leader of the organisation. They also played major role for expansion of the activities of the organisation during their underground period. Due to the repressive measures of the Government some of them were arrested and others were surrendered to the Government.

From this fact several observations can be made on the nature and character of the leadership of this organisation. It is also an undeniable fact that the true nature and character of the leader was always influenced by the social, political and economic environment of the area, where the revolutionary activities took place. In regard to the leadership of the "Meitei State Committee" it can be suggested that almost all the important leaders of this organisation was born and brought up in rural areas where the peasants constituted the major backbone of the society. So, these leaders had enjoyed a wonderful experience about the hard life of the peasant society which is regarded by many political philosophers as an important instrument for a complete transformation in every aspects of the existing society. From this angle it can be said that the leaders of the Meitei State Committee was the masters of the real hard life of the peasants and they had successfully explored and utilized the existing environmental situation as the tool of their revolutionary activities. In this respect it can also be observed that their original concept and thinking on the problems and grievances of the peasants was further sharpened by Late Hijam Irabot Singh who strongly advocated for the preservation of a separate political identity of Manipur and to establish a new society based on the principle of socialism. To materialize his objective into action he launched a left oriented armed revolutionary movement in 1948. His style of working and concept of revolutionary principles was the basic foundation for the establishment of this revolutionary organisation. It is true that all the important leaders of this organisation were once the active participants in the revolutionary movement of Hijam Irabot Singh. So, their mind and spirit were highly coloured by the idea of Manipur nationalism which was the brain child of late Irabot. So, due to this strong political influence of their late leader they again prepared to go to the same path for the preservation of the separate political identity of Manipur. From this fact it can be mentioned that the spirit, the idea and concept of revolution of the leadership of Meitei State Committee was a highly praiseworthy action on their part. Their emotional idea on the Manipuri nationalism was a noteworthy contribution to the people of Manipur in general.

However, since they were not able to get the facilities of proper modern education they had little knowledge about the highly technical and theoretical concept of the socialist revolution. As a result of this the leadership of Meitei State Committee was not able to equip properly their revolutionary idea with the theoretical concept of socialist revolution. Therefore due to the lack of knowledge their basic desire was not fully communicated to the common people. As a result of this their action and nature of the movement was branded by the elements of the existing administrative set-up in a totally different way and coloured them as a group of anti-social elements. It is mentioned that the Meitei State Committee was started as a revolutionary organisation after the establishment of an understanding with the Naga underground organisation. W. Tomba Singh, the leader of the organisation had categorically asserted that a successful revolution for the preservation of a separate identity of Manipur could be possible only with the help and co-operation of the hill people of the surrounding areas. He further said that this was the desire of his one time leader H. Irabot Singh and he wanted to continue this spirit and the idea should be communicated to the common people. But when the idea was prepared to translate into action and when the organisation was about to establish it seems that there were some lack of clarity in the minds of the leadership of this organisation. It is a known fact that the desire of the leadership was to launch a mass movement for the independence of Manipur and by involving all the people of the different community as a participant in their movement. However from the reality it is quite evident that their independent nature was overshadowed by the influence of 'Naga Underground Movement'. The earlier proposed name, the 'Manipur State Committee', was not accepted by the 'Naga Underground' organisation on the ground that since they fought for Naga people the new organisation should not cover all the hill people of Manipur. Therefore they asked the leaders to concentrate only in the valley areas. The arguments of the 'Naga Underground' was accepted by the leadership of this organisation and changed to "Meitei State Committee". There are a lot of questions to be discussed. This trend clearly shows the lack of maturity among the leadership of the organisation and it also indicates their level of awareness in the social and political life of the state. Perhaps the leaders of the Meitei State Committee was not fully awared of the basic objective of the 'Naga Underground' movement and their attitude towards the people of the valley area of Manipur. The change of name of the organisation from the "Manipur State Committee" to 'Meitei State Committee' had narrowed down the area of operation of the leadership of the organisation and on the other hand it has also created an impression that the leaders of this organisation were the believers of sectarian approach. This is the most tragic development in the approach of the leadership of this organisation. From this fact it can be observed that the leaders of the organisation were not very clear about the direction of the organisation and their level of understanding about the social and political relationship among the people of this State was also extremely low.

Another important feature in the character of the leadership of the Meitei State Committee was its policy of democratization in every decision of the organisation. The character of "authoritarian" elements was not visible in the working system among the leaders of Meitei State Committee. Every major decision was adopted and finalized in a very democratic way. Shri W. Tomba Singh, though he was the top Leader of the organisation, never took the advantage of the situation and position. In every matter he always took the majority opinions of the other members. This was a unique feature in the character of the leadership quality of Shri W. Tomba Singh. From this angle it can be suggested that the leadership character of Meitei State Committee was purely on the principle of 'democratic leadership'.

Apart from this the personal character of Shri W. Tomba Singh as a revolutionary leader was also another contributing factor for the rapid growth of the activities of the organisation. Shri W. Tomba Singh, despite so many limitations in his personnel life, was a true revolutionary leader. He never surrendered his principle of revolutionary spirit to his enemy. He never asked for any kind of assistance from the agents of the government. Instead he spent his remaining life as a simple and ordinary person of a peasant society. He never gave up his idea of revolutionary spirit till the last days of his life.

But unfortunately in case of the other leaders of the organisation, though they had a strong desire to bring a total change in the existing society, their mind was highly influenced by the principle of the individual interest. At the same time they were also not able to bear the burden of the economic grievances in their respective families. Therefore when the government offered them to take money under the rehabilitation programme they readily accepted it. Except Shri W. Tomba Singh, all the important leaders of the organisation received a sum of Rs. 2000 (Two thousand) from the government of Manipur. This is a clear evidence of the lack of maturity in the rank and files of the Meitei State Committee. On the other hand it can also be observed that such type of tendency which was developed in the minds of the leaders was nothing but simply it was due to the lack of understanding and knowledge about the real problem of the society and politics of the place to which they belonged. Because of the lack of intellectual depth the leaders of the Meitei State Committee was not able to influence and convince the educated youths of urban areas.

Whatever the case may be, if the totality of the leadership of the Meitei State Committee is to be analyzed, it can be safely concluded that the leadership of this organisation had set a very good example of how to carry the masses with an ideological foundation to the path of a revolutionary movement. In spite of so many technical drawbacks the commitments of the leadership, sense of sacrifice, degree of their patriotism and their strong desire to establish a new society based on socialism cannot be easily ignored and overshadowed by a mere mistake. On top of this their attempt to bring the masses from such a social condition where no advantageous facilities were available for a mass uprising cannot be ignored. Their spirit and attempt are really a commendable one and their sense of Manipuri nationalism and concept of unity and oneness among the different groups of people has laid a new foundation for the people of younger generation in their attempt to maintain the unity of the people. In one way they may be treated as a more advanced, more militant, more decisive elements of revolutionized people. It is said that "Those who take up arms or who become organizers in the initial stage of popular guerrilla struggle are not, therefore a minority of 'agitators'.[20] so the leadership of the Meitei State Committee and their organizational activities were not separated from the people. And at the same time they also got the support of the masses. But the only problem faced by the leadership was that due to lack of the understanding of the existing outlook of the common people they were not able to carry all the people of every section of the society within the orbit of their organisation and ideology.

## UNITED NATIONAL LIBERATION FRONT (UNLF) (PRE-R.G.M. PERIOD)

The deep-rooted ideological concept of 'Manipuri nationalism' was the only inner positive strength of the United National Liberation Front (UNLF). To bring a unity among the people of Manipur and to identify themselves as one group, was the basic motto of this organisation. The idea of 'Pan-Mongoloid' concept was the clear indication of the concept of the organisation. The Pan Manipuri Youth League (PANMYL) which was branded as an over ground organisation of the United National Liberation Front (UNLF) has defined the term Manipuri as "all the original inhabitants of Manipur, including those who have left their homes and are now living outside who follow the traditional Manipuri way of life irrespective of religion and language; people of the same racial and cultural origin with the people of Manipur who though residing outside Manipur still identify themselves as Manipuris."[21] The objective of PANMYL was observed as a 'styling show', 'flamboyant concept' and 'fantastically utopian idea' and an 'ambitious outlook'.[22] The idea for the establishment of the concept of oneness among the Manipuris which was initiated at the third session of Nikhil Hindu Manipuri Mahasabha at Mandalay by Hijam Irabot Singh was again flourished by the leadership of this organisation particularly among the younger generation people of this State. It is a known fact that the United National Liberation Front was established at the initiative of the well-educated people. This was a unique feature of the organisation. As has already been mentioned above, the United National Liberation Front was a product of both some educated young people and some people of middle class who was the old guards of the society of Manipur. The contribution of different professional groups in the formation of this organisation like journalists, dancers, medical practitioners, teachers, lawyers, etc. cannot be just overlooked very easily. In one way they were the backbone of the organisation and their idea and concept was the basic ideological foundation of the organisation. So, from these facts it is quite clear that different personalities were actively involved and participated in the formation of the organisation. Among them there were two important leaders.

One was Arambam Samarendra Singh who was the founder general secretary and main architect of the organisation and another was Oinam Sudhirkumar Singh who was a youth leader of the organisation. In one way and from their activities it can be observed that these two personalities may be regarded as the key players and the contributing factors for any type of eventuality faced by the organisation in their future course of action.

Constantine observed Samarendra as "an unimpressive person, impassive but intent."[23] Arambam Samarendra Singh was born and brought up in a highly respected aristocratic middle class family of the urban society. He was born on 12th July, 1935. After passing class ten from Johnstone High School he did his B.A. at Dhanamanjuri College, Manipur and passed M.A. from Poona (Pune) University in the year 1963. During his undergraduate student life he was actively involved and participated in the activities of National Cadet Corps (NCC) which was established in the year 1955-56 at D.M. College. He was the first student who became a Senior Under Officer of the National Cadet Corps. Apart from this he also actively participated in the students' movements in Manipur. Before going to Poona for further study he served as a teacher at Luwangsangbam School along with Pramod Singh from Thangmeiband. Samarendra Singh was born and brought up in an environment which was greatly influenced by the pedigree of different social elements. His grandfather Arambam Meino Singh, the first Sub-Inspector of Police was a staunch colonial officer who was greatly influenced by the practices and principles of the way of the life of the English people and a man of authoritarian character. Because of this he was highly respected by the people of his time and he was also an influential man in the administration of the state. The grandmother of Samarendra was Rajkumari Khomdonsana, the youngest daughter of Maharaja Surchandra Singh who was deposed from the throne by the Palace Revolt of 1890. It is mentioned that she was a lady who strongly believed in the principle of the preservation of the national identity of Manipur. She was greatly influenced by the sense of patriotism and nationalism of the royal blood in her level of understanding. The father of Samarendra Singh was Arambam Dorendarajit Singh. His nature and character was a complete reverse of his father. He was a well-educated man of his time. He was a reknown poet, dramatist and Sanskrit scholar. He possessed a very good quality of humble character and very accommodative. At the same time he was also a social worker. Jamini Devi, the mother of A. Samarendra Singh, was a woman who was strongly influenced by the orthodoxy of traditional concept and practices of Hindu religion. She was a very good house wife and always looked after the welfare of her family, her husband and her children. She also possessed a very good quality of cool and calmness but very fast in her decision. She is a devoted mother who acted as main pillar to the cause of her son.[24]

Indeed A. Samarendra Singh was a man of complex personality. He was a thinker, a writer, a sport lover, a great playwright and good social worker. Over and above he was a champion of Manipuri nationalism. His idea of nationalism, his love for Manipur, his only dream to foster and promote the cultural identity of this country was clearly reflected in every inch of his work and writing. From these evidences it may be suggested that he had a good genetical influence from the different environments of the older members of his family. A deep-rooted clear-cut ideological foundation was also another important advantageous position of Samarendra. With the help of his ideological background he was able to impart the idea of Manipuri nationalism and the concept of oneness among the different ethnic groups of this region and the feeling for the preservation and maintenance of the identity of the people of this state among the common people particularly to the educated people of the younger generation. He was a soft-spoken man. He never used harsh word to anybody nor gave any type of negative criticism against the work of any individual or group. On top of this he had a wonderful quality to identify the right person for the right job. This is also another essential qualification, which is to be possessed by every leader. The leader must have capability to give the assignment to the right persons otherwise he or she cannot be a good leader. Another advantageous quality of A. Samerendro was his simplicity. With the help of this quality he was able to mix up with any people of any ethnic group of different ages. Therefore he gave an opportunity to all the people to get the privilege to get access to him very easily. Therefore the elder people had a very high opinion about Samarendra. It is also said that Samarendra had a high respect for all the different professional classes. But he never encouraged bureaucratic nature. Another quality of Samarendra was his relationship with all the people of the surrounding hill areas of

Manipur. One of his close observer said that during his revolutionary movement Hijam Irabot Singh had good relationship mainly with Kabuis and Kukis whereas Samaredra tried to establish good relationship with all the different ethnic groups of the surrounding hill areas.[25] In a way, from the evidences of his work, it can be said that Arambam Samarendra Singh was a man who belonged to the categories of 'born revolutionaries'. His idea of revolution was not confined to the concept of armed revolutionary movement alone. He also made a serious attempt to bring a revolutionary change in the social, cultural and literary outlook of the people of Manipur in the tone of the on going process of development in the other parts of the globe. It is also mentioned that the idea of Manipuri nationalism of Samarendra was further strengthened by Captain Harnet, an army officer of India. Before coming to Manipur he was serving in the royal court of the Nizam of Hyderabad as A.D.C. During that time he had a very good experience of how the Nizam of Hyderabad tried to save and preserve the separate political identity of Hyderabad State from the violent pressure of the Indian government. He narrated this untold story to some of his N.C.C. cadets. He even asked them to make an attempt to foster the national identity of the Manipuris. Such type of events also greatly encouraged Samarendra to strengthen his original idea of Manipuri nationalism.[26] Another important feature of Samarendra was his outlook towards the womenfolk of the Manipur state. He always said that the social position of the women should be highly respected and distinctive cultural identity of the women should be honoured. His concept of women had clearly reflected in his writings and drama. In short it can be said that Arambam Samarendra was a great revolutionary ideologue and leader after Hijam Irabot Singh. He was a true devotee to the cause in which he believed. His body and mind was completely espoused to the principle of revolution and for the welfare of the people. He was also a humanist and he was always prepared to extend all the possible help to the needy people both collective and individual. Another important noteworthy achievement in the revolutionary principle of Arambam Samarendra was that during revolutionary period he never surrendered to the government. This is a unique feature in the revolutionary character of the leader. He came out over ground only when the government declared a general amnesty to the revolutionaries.

Oinam Sudhirkumar Singh was another important leading personality who always played a vital role in the revolutionary process of this organisation. He was regarded as the youth leader. He was born in February 1942 in a very poor family at Singjamei Oinam Thingel area in the southern side of Imphal city. The name of his father was Oinam Ibomcha Singh, a local astrologer. So, according to his profession he was popularly known in his surrounding areas as 'Mangol Panji'. His mother was Loitongbam Ningol Oinam Ongbi Nupimacha Devi. Sudhirkumar Singh was the second son of his parents. The name of the eldest brother is Dhanendrajit and two other elder sisters were Chandrakala and Amurei Devi. His younger sister's name is Maingoubi Devi and his youngest brother's name is Shantikumar. He started his early education from Aheibam Leikai L.P. School. He completed his M.E. course from Moirangkhom M.E. School and in the year 1959 he passed Matric from Johnstone School in the first division. It is said that at the beginning he had not taken much interest in the education but fro n the high School level his hidden talent and character of a brainy student could be noticed by his fellow students. After passing class IX (nine) he became an extra ordinarily student. One of his old friends said that late Sudhirkumar was able to write and speak the English language so fluently that even the senior student had praised him for his gifted talent. Apart from this he also possessed some interesting natural qualifications. He had a high degree of sense of humour and human touch. He was always ready to extend all sorts of possible help to the needy persons. It is also said that he had a strong quality to debate and his logic was also very sharp. The degree of his argument in very issue was very high and nature of his argument was quite authoritative and assertive. In spite of all this his technique of free mixing with any person of different character was also quite interesting. It is mentioned that because of this qualification he was able to mix with peoples without having any problem. In short, Sudhir possessed a rare quality of leadership. Besides this, he had a wonderful commanding personality as well as he was also a man of revolting type of personality. It is said that his revolting type of personality might be genetically inherited from his father. That his father 'Mangol Panji' was man of a strong negative attitude. In every issue and matter he always looked with a critical eye and he was very much rigid in his decision. Such type of character of his father was also reflected in the nature of O. Sudhirkumar Singh. Indeed he was a man of straight forward nature and there was no internal contradiction in his ideas and thought. On top of this he was a man of wide reading. His friends regarded him as a terrific reader. He had gone through all the books particularly the books written on the works of revolutionary leaders of the world. As a result of this he had full knowledge and information on every vital issue which was more or less related with social, political and economic life of the region particularly of Manipur.

But after passing I.Sc. in the year 1961, O. Sudhirkumar began to make a complete change in the trend of his bright academic career. Just after passing I.Sc., perhaps it might be due to lack of financial support from the family, he stopped to continue his study and joined in the service of the department of Statistical Bureau as a regular employee. He was in the office for about two or three years. When he was in service he passed B.A. by appearing, perhaps as a private candidate, from Imphal College. It is said that he passed B.A. when he was posted at Kakching.[27] Then he left the service due to quarrel with the head of the department. According to an information he joined the service not as a regular employee. So, he was not able to continue the sevice.[28] It is mentioned that from the very beginning Sudhir had a strong desire to do something for the establishment of a separate identity of Manipur. He expressed his desire and intention to some of his close friends. He even asked them to work together.[29] After leaving the service of the government he became an assistant teacher in a school at Somdal Village in Ukhrul District. But some people were of the view that he was at Somdal village for a specific purpose because at that time he was already an active member of the organisation. It is also mentioned that his growing idea of Manipuri nationalism and desire to establish a separate identity of Manipur might be influenced by Arambam Samarendra Singh as both of them had closely associated before the establishment of this revolutionary organisation.[30] One of his close friends said that during his early days of his life Shri Sudhir Singh did not have the time to enjoy any type of youthful days as he had already espoused to the idea of the revolutionary principle and became one of the torch bearers of the spirit of Manipuri nationalism.

The other important leaders who had actively participated and contributed to the cause of the movement and the construction of an ideological foundation of the organisation were (1) Shri Kalalung, (2) Shri Singsheet, (3) Dr. Manimohon, (4) Shri Pramod, (5) Shri N. Pahari, etc. They also played a very important role for the promotion and strengthening of the organisation at their best ability.

As stated above the real picture of the character and nature of the leader of any type of revolutionary movement is greatly influenced by the surrounding political, social and economic environment. In case of the United National Liberation Front, most of the leaders were urban educated middle class family. The educated middle class here signify the new group of persons who received higher education through the medium of English and who engaged in any profession that grew as a result of western education. Being members of the middle class family they have got the opportunity to understand the social and economic problems of the people both from the lowest to the highest level of the social strata of the country. In addition to this most of the leaders of the organisation was of a new educated elite group which emerged just after the integration of Manipur into India. Their greatest advantage was that they had enjoyed the opportunity to witness the whole drama of the merger of Manipur into India. Perhaps they were under the impression that the merger of Manipur would bring a positive impact in Manipur. But when the things had changed beyond their expectation they immediately started the idea of the establishment of separate identity of Manipur on the basis of Manipuri nationalism. This aspect is the most noteworthy contributions of the leaders of the U.N.L.F. In addition to this and because of their educational background, the people of older generation had a high regard to their wisdom, integrity and sense of nationalism. Taking this opportunity they could easily influence the desire of the people. On top of this, leadership of the organisation was not confined alone in the valley areas. The people from the hill areas were also actively involved and they also gave a very good contribution on the way of strengthening the position of the organisation in their respective areas. Therefore the idea of collective leadership was very much involved in the revolutionary movement of UNLF.

This idea of collective leadership was very much clearly reflected in their organizational system and their revolutionary planning was carried out through a highly systematic hierarchical structure. There were two main bodies of the organisation i.e. Executive Committee and Coordinating Committee. The Executive was constituted by 9(nine) members including office bearers. This was the highest decision making body of the organisation and all the members were also given a very important responsible positions of the organisation. The Coordinating Committee was constituted by 30(thirty) members. From this structural position it can be observed that the UNLF has got the character of democratic leadership system. But due to some unavoidable conditions the real character of the leadership of this organisation was not able to come out to the visible point of the common people. It was mainly due to their internal problem. The internal crisis, in fact, was not directly related with the tendency on the issue of the capturing of the top leadership of the organisation. It was more or less related with the party's approach and style of movement. There are two types of approach of the leadership i.e. elite leadership and organizational leadership. The first one is concerned with the explanation of leadership in top position and the organizational leadership is mainly concerned with the qualities required of an ideal leader in charge of the group and organisation. It is observed that the first category deals with leadership as a phenomenon in all societies and has been the favourable subject of political philosopher and the other one deals with leadership as being a set of attributes which are required for achieving organizational objectives.[31] So, the internal crisis of the party was very much related with the crisis of these two types of approach in the top level of the party. As mentioned above, one of the top leaders of UNLF, Shri Arambam Samarendra Singh, was indeed a thinker and a philosopher. No doubt he was the main architect of the whole theoretical foundation of this revolutionary party. He was very cool and considerate and his only desire was to carry the whole masses within the orbit of the ideological concept of the party. From this fact it can be suggested that he was a leader of the masses. Whereas his junior colleague, Oinam Sudhir Singh, whom the other members regarded him as a youth leader was an action oriented man. He believed that the people's positive response would come out only when the organisation showed its action. Except this there were no difference of opinion among the leadership of the party. As a whole, the leadership pattern of the United National Liberation Front was based purely on the basis of the collective and democratic principle. However. though the organisation had enjoyed the opportunity to get the service of the well-educated persons as members but because of the contradiction in the approach they could not display the real character of the leadership pattern to the masses. Therefore, since the United National Liberation Front was not able to demonstrate their revolutionary activities into action the real portrait of the identity of the character of leadership was reached to the knowledge of the people with great confusion and complexity. Constantine wrote, "Both however agreed on the objective, namely the establishment of a Republic of Manipur as well as the means, the violent overthrow of state apparatus. The difference was over the tempo of action. Sudhir wanted quick and spectacular deals while Samarendra advocated slow but steady and firm acion".[32]

## REVOLUTIONARY GOVERNMENT OF MANIPUR (R.G.M.)

The establishment of "Revolutionary Government of Manipur" (R.G.M.) as a revolutionary organisation was an immediate outcome of the result of the internal crisis of the United National Liberation Front. The leader of this organisation was Shri Oinam Sudhirkumar Singh. As has been mentioned above Sudhirkumar Singh was a man having action-oriented nature. So he was not satisfied with the go-slow nature of some important leaders of the UNLF. On this basic issue he came out from the organisation and established the RGM as a revolutionary party on the same line and ideological principle of the previous organisation. No doubt so far the organizational structure was concerned the R.G.M. also adopted the principle of democratic approach by constituting an executive body and different assignment was given to all the members of the body. But if the nature and working style of the organisation is to be analyzed it can be observed that the whole working and nature of the adoption of policy was entirely in the hand of the top leader. Indeed, it was not a surprising development because the party itself was formed very hurriedly due to the internal crisis of their mother organisation. From these evidences it can be suggested that the leadership pattern of the organisation was not very much different from the authoritarian type of leadership. As already stated above under the principle of this type of leadership the policies and directive were determined by the leader and the dictated task would be carried out by the co-workers.

Apart from Sudhirkumar other important leaders of RGM were N. Bisheshwor Singh and R.K. Sanajaoba Singh. They also played a major role for the fulfillment of their plan with a positive result. Since the nature and character and environmental background of O. Sudhirkumar Singh, the top leader of the organisation, has already been mentioned above there is no point of further discussion about his background. However, his authoritarian nature of leadership was severely criticized even by his own people when the party got a jolt under the oppressive measure of the government. In their confessional statement they even said that they did not know anything about the aim and objective of the organisation. They simply accepted when they were offered to give armed training in East Pakistan. They even lamented that these people ruined their life.[33] Some ex-members said that they were arrested by the police because of the highly ambitious and impatient nature of Sudhirkumar. His greedy aim to capture power bought all these catastrophic result to the course of the movement.[34] Whatever the case may be from the evidences of the process of their movement it can be observed that the majority of the members of this organisation was not very clear about the nature in the approach of the party. They were not even clear about the aim and objective of the party. It seems that everything was arranged in a very haphazard way. The large scale arrest of the volunteers of the organisation was indeed a gross mistake on the part of the leadership. It shows the lack of experience and wisdom in the process of the art of decision-making. From the circumstantial evidences it can be established as a fact that the recruitment of volunteers or members of the party was done not in a proper way. It means that the persons who were involved in the activity were not properly well equipped with the knowledge of ideology and objective of the party. They became the members of the party only through the sentimental aspects on the issue of the anti-Indian feeling. Except this, they knew nothing about the other aspect of the organisation to which they belonged. From this fact it can also be observed that the leaders of the organisation both in their approach and mentality were not fully espoused to the theoretical concept of the revolution.

But in spite of so many drawbacks in the nature of the leadership of the organisation, the establishment of Revolutionary Government of Manipur and its revolutionary activities brought a new light to those persons who made a serious attempt to translate the vision of an independent Manipur which was founded by the old guards of the revolution into action. The mistakes committed by the leader or leaders of the organisation gave a new lesson to the new generation of leadership. It is said that the R.G.M. failed because, there were two lines of struggle among the leadership. One was the roads to revivalism and another was Marxist road.[35] But this observation was developed only when some of the erstwhile leader of R.G.M. established a new revolutionary organisation. Therefore it is very difficult to establish a hypothesis that there was an ideological conflict among the leadership of R.G.M. In addition to that this revolutionary organisation was established under sole initiative of Oinam Sudhirkumar Singh. From this fact and as it has already been mentioned above the leadership nature of the R.G.M. was not totally different from the 'Authoritarian type of leadership'.

## PEOPLE'S LIBERATION ARMY UNIT (EASTERN REGION) 1978-1981

The significant character and a unique ideological feature of the People's Liberation Army Unit (Eastern Region) has already been explained in the previous chapter. Indeed, the idea of the establishment of a separate political identity of the entire states of North-Eastern Region of India and the establishment of a new society based on the socialist pattern of society which is the basic principle of Marxism was also another unprecedented political and ideological development in the region and a major contribution of the People's Liberation Army Unit (Eastern Region). In their official papers the PLA (Eastern Region) strongly asserted for the improvement of the social and economic positions of workers and peasants which are the main pillars of any society. They also believed that these two elements in the society are the most important tools to the success of the socialist revolution. On the basic principle of this ideological foundation and after failure of their predecessors the organizer of the party started and carried out the revolutionary activities of the People's Liberation Army Unit (Eastern Region) with great care and effectiveness. The historical background of the establishment of the organisation and the course of the activities is also mentioned very clearly in the other chapter. From these evidences it can be observed that the nature of the leadership of the People's Liberation Army Unit (Eastern Region) has got a basic difference from the leadership of other revolutionary organizations. In the case of this organisation the whole revolutionary activities was carried on under the charismatic personality of a leader.

Nameirakpam Bisheshwor Singh was the founder leader of the People's Liberation Army Unit (Eastern Region). He was born at Naorem Leikai in a very poor family. He started his early career in the midst of extreme economic hardship in his family. His father's name was N. Khorobi Singh and mother's name was Mando Devi. His father was a hard working man. Apart from this he was also involved in labour co-operative movement. It is said that he was the secretary of the Naorem Leikai Labour Contract Society. His mother was a very good housewife and she always paid attention to the welfare of her children. Bisheshwor had two sisters and one brother. He was the eldest son of his parents and other are (i) N. Sur Devi, (ii) Modhuchandra who expired as an underground activist, and (iii) his younger sister Bimota Devi who is still actively participating in the revolutionary movement.

N. Bisheshwor Singh started his early education from Canchipur High School and passed class X from this school in the year 1965. He continued his general study at Imphal College up to Pre-University level (P.U.C.). It is said that due to the acute financial difficulty in the family he was not in a position to continue his study as a regular student. However he had a strong will to continue his study. So, he began to work as a construction labour in the daytime. In spite of his best attempt and efforts he was not completely free from the struggle of economic hardship that became increasingly tough. According to a journalistic investigation report of a journal it is recorded that the moment he completed B.A. 1st year course he got an offer of monthly stipend of Rs. 80 (Eighty) to take a course in ceramics in Calcutta.[36] It was a serious moment in his life. On the one hand he was continuously attacked by the acute financial problem of his family and on the other if he opted in favour of the training course that would be the end of the continuation of his general study. Finally he opted for the training course. It is further reported that after having finished the course in the year 1968 at the ceramic institute in Jadavpur he came back to Manipur with the hope to make a living out of the skill he had acquired. First he made a series of attempts to get a suitable post in the Government job. Since he was not able to get the opportunity he had decided to start a small ceramics unit of his own. Therefore in order to start his small-scale industry he applied for a meager amount of Rs. 5000 (Five Thousand) for a loan. But contrary to this report and as mentioned by his close friends and relatives, Bisheshwor, after passing P.U.C. went to Solan in Himachal Pradesh to get the training of 'Clinical Thermometer'. He went there along with two other persons. The trade of the training course of other two persons was not known. The journalistic report about the attempt of Bisheshwor to get a suitable government job and to seek financial help from the state was strongly refuted by his friends and relatives. They said that he never made any such attempt from the government. But they also agreed that before he came into contact with the activists of the United National Liberation Front (UNLF), gradually he started to lose faith in himself and very soon he was in the midst of disillusionment. While this was the situation he began to have touch with some members of the UNLF and became a member of this organisation. It is said that he joined revolutionary movement with the blessing of his own mother. With tears in his eyes Bisheshwor said that he was seen off by his mother up to the area of Goddess Panthoibi of Naorem Leikai and bid adieu by touching his head. She wished him success. Then from this moment he began to change his career and outlook as an important revolutionary activist. Gradually he was able to establish a close relationship and understanding with O. Sudhirkumar Singh who was an important youth leader of U.N.L.F. Then just after the split of UNLF he was on the side of Sudhirkumar and began to take an important responsibility in the revolutionary activities of R.G.M. which was established under the leadership of O. Sudhirkumar Singh. He was arrested in 1972 while returning from one of the missions in East Pakistan (Bangladesh). The birth of Bangladesh became a severe cause for the failure of R.G.M. because just after this new political development all their communication were totally cut off and ultimately it led to the arrest of all the leaders of the organisation. After the declaration of general amnesty all the members who were actively involved in the revolutionary activities came out from the jail. Some of them began to accept the offer promised by the state government either in cash or in kind and began to settle a new life. Bisheshwor did not accept the offer and remained as defiant as ever and distanced himself from the other ex-R.G.M. activists who opted for a peaceful life. Then after spending for a very short period of time, without doing any revolutionary activities, he again established another revolutionary organisation i.e., People's Liberation Army Unit (Eastern Region). The establishment of this organisation may be treated as a major achievement of Bisheshwor because in this organisation he had the opportunity to enjoy the maximum privilege to express his ideas and desire for the cause of the people. Thus Bisheshwor was able to demonstrate himself bot . as a revolutionary activist and leader till he was arrested by the Indian army in the year 1981. By analyzing his early period of life and on the basis of their information they further observed that Bisheshwor Singh "might well have been a potter instead of a militant insurgent leader if he had his way. That was what he wanted to be."[37]

The nature of leadership pattern was totally different from the other organizations. No doubt the organisation in order to carry the revolutionary activities, had constituted a small apex body of seven members. It was known as 'Executive Body'. But the nature of the style of working of the body is to be studied very carefully. It can be suggested that everything was done under the sole personality of the top leader i.e., Bisheshwor Singh. The elements of the spirit of collective leadership was also there but in practice it was not fully implemented. It is also an undeniable fact that during his period, the whole revolutionary activities of P.L.A. was going on under his personality. From this angle some people regarded him as an undisputed legendary leader of the People's Liberation Army Unit (Eastern Region). Whatever the case may be, it can be suggested that in the working of the organisation everything was carried out under his leadership. This type of leadership pattern is called 'charismatic leadership'. The element of charismatic authority is present in all forms of leadership but Max Weber said "the predominantly charismatic leader is distinguished from other leaders by his capacity to inspire and sustain loyalty and devotion to him personally, apart from his office or status"[38] He further said that a man of charismatic personality shall have the capacity to imbue with a sense of mission, felt as divinely inspired which he communicate to his followers. He breaks precedents and creates new ones and so is revolutionary. He seems to flourish in time of disturbances and distress.[39] Edward Shils also said that "the charismatic powers is a creator of a new order as well as breaker of routine order".[40] From these observations it can also be suggested that the charismatic leader is able to communicate to his followers a sense of continuity between himself and his mission and their legendary heroes and their missions. Indeed, the mobilization of the popular support would be the only behaviour of any leader. But the only difference of the charismatic leader is the role of the myth in validating his authority. Claude Levy Strauss said "since a myth remain the same as long as it is felt as such he and his claims are legitimated by his ability to draw on himself the mantle of myth".[41] In this connection it is also observed that "the charismatic leader is charismatic because in the breakdown of other means of legitimizing authority, he is able to evoke and associated with himself the symbol of his culture."[42] The charismatic leadership is also known as ideal relationship in which the relationship is characterized by love or affection.

As has been mentioned above the feature of the leadership pattern of the organisation was based on the individual leadership principle. In fact, N. Bisheshwor Singh was all in all in the party. He was the supreme authority in every organizational matter. Apart from his organizational leadership he was also a theorist and an ideologue of the party. Due to the multifaceted role in the process of the growth and promotion of the party his colleagues affectionately paid their respect by calling him 'Oza' (teacher). Inside the party Bisheshwor was known among the members as 'Oza Achouba' (Big teacher). In every official papers of the party the members used two terms i.e. 'Oza' (teacher) and 'Luching Puren' (Supreme Leader). Thus he was able to establish a very good relationship with his comrades in the party. Besides this, during his revolutionary days his name was the talk of every young people. Everybody had an impression that he would definitely bring a new change in the social and political life of the people and the state. And even a myth was created that he had undergone plastic surgery in Lhasa to alter his facial look so that he could not be recognized. Even the officers and sepoys of the Indian army also had this impression. So, when he was in the hand of the army they had a serious doubt whether he was the real Bisheshwor or not. When he said that he was Bisheshwor Col. Sinha did not believe his word and began to ask so many questions including the whereabout of Bisheshwor. To Col.

Sinha the present nature of Bisheshwor was a total contrast from his belief. He said that he (Bisheshwor) "hardly looked like a raving conspirator, a militant insurgency leader. He was not even carrying a gun. With his wide nose, disheveled hair and sagging eyes he looked even teddy bearish".[43] Indeed, Bisheshwor was branded in the minds of the people as the symbol of the deep rooted conditions of poverty, neglect and despire in Manipur and the anger against it. His emphatatic slogan for the change of a new society based on a new independent political identity makes him a kind of folk hero for the underprivileged not only of Manipur but of the entire region. It is mentioned that nobody believed in the news of the arrest of Bisheshwor because to the people he was like 'Phantom or superman come alive indestructible'.[44] Such type of myth spontaneously took away much of the mystery and romanticism that were associated with him in the minds of the people.

Whatsoever it be, from the pattern of leadership and nature of the organisation it can be observed that the form of leadership of the People's Liberation Army Unit (Eastern Region) was entirely based on the model of charismatic leadership. From the analysis of the nature of other members of the organisation it can be observed that in their mind their leader. 'N. Bisheshwor Singh was the organisation', and 'their organisation was Bisheshwor'. Thus through his charismatic strength Bisheshwor could legitimized his authority inside the organisation.

However the working pattern of the organisation is to be studied. It can also be suggested that there were some elements of democratic leadership nature in the real working system. It is mentioned that though N. Bisheshwor Singh was the supreme authority in the party he never misused his position. He did not make any final decision without consulting his core group. Those members who received armed and ideological training in Lahsa were the core group of the organisation. The security personals called them 'elite group'. These members enjoyed the maximum opportunity to exercise their independent nature in the process of the development of the organisation. But this does not mean that they had the power to defy the decision of the leader. They cannot go beyond the code of conduct of the organisation. From this fact it can be said that there were elements of internal democracy in the functioning of the party. Whereas so far the leadership pattern is concerned the People's Liberation Army Unit (Eastern Region) was based entirely on the charismatic leadership.

## PEOPLE'S REVOLUTIONARY PARTY OF KANGLEIPAK (PREPAK) 1977-1985

"The fate of Kangleipak should be determined by the Kangleicha (sons of Kanglei). The people of the present generation should not forget that she was a sovereign state and this political status was maintained systematically by the forefathers of Kanglei right from the time immemorial".[45] This is the basic motto of this revolutionary organisation. On the basis of this belief some enthusiastic youths had established the 'People's Revolutionary Party of Kangleipak' (PREPAK) with an objective to establish Manipur as an independent country outside the political boundary of the Indian Union. In order to have a smooth sailing in their revolutionary movement the PREPAK had identified two important elements in the society as the main hurdle in their positive approach. According to them the class enemy and neo-colonialist imperialist force are the two important obstacles in their ongoing process of successful revolution. So, PREPAK strongly emphasized for the establishment of a classless society which is free from the oppressive tendencies of neo-colonialist imperialist force. They also claimed that their "revolution is people's revolution" and "party is making rooms for all people".[46] They also shared the agony of the people who suffered under the government of colonial rule. PREPAK always treated the present government of India as the colonial administration. So, as it has already been stated above the only objective of the organisation was to launch armed revolution in order to save those people who have forfeited their real identity and to establish a classless society. They further viewed that there is a basic difference between the independence of the country and the independence of the people. At the same time, they also strongly asserted that PREPAK is not in favour of the restoration of the monarchical form of government wherein only a few people had the privilege to enjoy the maximum opportunity in the administration against the common interest of the general mass. They said that in order to carry the administration for the welfare of the people there should be a party of the people. One of the important objectives of the party was to give the maximum security to the people and as a duty army have to obey the order of the people. PREPAK strongly believed that the barrel of the gun of the army should not be able to rule the people. They should be guided by the party of the people. To give freedom to the people was the only pledge of the organisation. They also claimed that the 'Red Army' would give freedom to the people and they would make Manipur a sovereign independent country based on the principle of the classless society. The party also asked the people of different ethnic groups in Manipur to take share in the revolution. The party further asserted that they (ethnic groups) are the genuine revolutionaries, because they are the highest exploited class[47] and without them no successful armed revolution could be launched. With these clear objectives the People's Revolutionary Party of Kangleipak was established by a small group of enthusiastic young people.

Among these enthusiastic youths, the most important revolutionary personality was Rajkumar Tullachandra Singh. The contributory role played by him in the process of the formation of the organisation and his sense of dedication and sacrifice for the growth of the party was the most important noteworthy aspect of the organisation. Shri R.K. Tullachandra Singh was born on Friday, the 4th December, 1953,[48] at Lourungpurel Leikai Thangmeiband near D.M. College in Imphal. He was the third son of the seven children of his parents. His father was Rajkumar Lochon Singh who was a teacher of L.P. school and his mother was Chingsubam Ningol Rajkumar Ongbi Priyosakhi Devi. The names of their children are: 1) Rajkumar Tullachandra Singh, 2) Rajkumari Kalapati Devi, 3) Rajkumari Rashesori Devi, 4) Rajkumar Modhuchandra Singh, 5) Rajkumar Chitrasen Singh, 6) Rajkumari Dhanamanjuri Devi, and 7) Rajkumari Mukabali Devi. Shri Rajkumar Tullachandra Singh started his early education from Thengmeiband Primary and M.E. School, Khoyathong. Then in the year 1972 he passed class X from Ramlal Paul High School. After passing matric he went to Orissa and passed intermediate class from Cuttuck Christian College, Cuttuck. After this there were some irregularities in his study. From there he came to Calcutta and took admission in American Business Centre. But he could not complete the course. Then he came back to Manipur and took admission in D.M. College of Arts and Commerce as a student of

Political Science. Then in the year 1977 he passed M.A. in political science from the Jawaharlal Nehru University Centre of Post Graduate Study, Imphal.

It is mentioned that R.K. Tullachandra started his childhood career as a very simple and humble lad. He was loved by every people of his locality. It is said that perhaps his active involvement in every social activity of the locality might be the reason for having the opportunity to get the love and affection of the people particularly from the elders of the locality. It is also said that he was very much fond of small children and he was always accompanied with them. Sometimes he narrated many stories which could give knowledge to them. Some of his old friends observed that his idea of patriotism and sense of Manipuri nationalism might have been influenced by his father. They said that in his best limited knowledge his father had always expressed his strong desire to maintain and protect the distinctive political identity of the Manipuri people. It is said that Tullachandra started to think for the welfare of the downtrodden people of Manipur right from his class six standard.[49] Gradually he began to show his leadership quality from the time of high school level. He began to participate in every movement launched by the students' community and when he was in Ramlal Paul High School he was actively involved in the organisation of students' community. He was the Parliamentary Secretary of the Student's Union of this school and became an active member of All Manipur Students' Union (AMSU) and later he became the Acting General Secretary of AMSU. It is said that he was able to witness the real scene of the worst conditions of workers in the factory when he was in Calcutta. For about six months he roamed all the important areas of Calcutta and tried to witness the real problem of the workers. Thus from this experience he was able to know the importance of class struggle and gradually entered into the ideological aspects of Marxism. With this vast experiences of knowledge Tullachandra decided to launch a mass movement for the establishment of an independent Manipur on the foundation of classless society. Accordingly, on the 19th September, 1976 with the co-operation of some of his close friends he established the 'Young Universe Manipur'.[50] Through this organisation he prepared a deep-rooted infrastructure for a large-scale armed revolutionary movement in Manipur. After having all the basic infrastructures for an armed revolutionary movement he established

People's Revolutionary Party of Kangleipak (PREPAK) on the 9th October, 1976.

The biggest asset of R.K. Tullachandra Singh as a revolutionary leader was his strong commitment to the ideology he espoused and principle in which he believed. Inside the party other members regarded him as an undisputed charismatic leader. Despite the many physical hurdles in the process of his revolutionary activities he had never shown any sign of moral degradation rather he tried to give any type of moral booster and encouragement to his revolutionary comrades. The other leaders of the party were 1) A. Dhiren, 2) Kabikanta Sharma, 3) Kritibabu Mangang, etc. Like Tullachandra they had also rendered a significant contribution towards the strengthening of their organisation. With the help of their sincere efforts this revolutionary organisation was able to move forward with many armed activities.

From the above evidence it can be observed that the leadership pattern of the organisation was based absolutely on collective leadership. Whatever decisions they adopted were purely on the line of democratic principle. This was clearly evidenced by the official pamphlets and leaflets of the party. Although Rajkumar Tullachandra Singh was the main architect[2] in the process of the formation of the party he never showed any type of authoritarian leadership nature in the whole process of the working of the party. Every important decision was always taken by the highest apex body of the party. Another important feature of the nature of the leadership of the party was their strict principle in respect of the working system of every department. Important decision of every department was taken by the respective leaders. So, a free hand and full responsibility was given to the respective departments. From this also it is quite visible about the democratic leadership factor of the party. Therefore the decentralization system of the working of the party is a clear reflection of the principle of the system of democratic leadership.

## KANGLEIPAK COMMUNIST PARTY (K.C.P.)

As has already been mentioned above the Kangleipak Communist Party (K.C.P.) was established with the sole objective to emancipate the peasants and workers who were suffering under the "colonial rule of Indian government"[51] and to liberate Manipur (Kangleipak). Another objective of the party was to establish a classless society by eliminating all the enemy agents who were actively involved in the administration. Under this ideological concept and political objective of the independence of Manipur the leaders and active volunteers of K.C.P. also participated in the process of the revolutionary movements of Manipur. It has already been mentioned above that the Kangleipak Communist Party was started with the initiative of some dedicated persons. Among them Shri Ibohanbi Singh also actively participated as volunteers in the revolutionary movement of Manipur State Committee. From this active involvement he got the idea of a need for a total change in the whole social political and economic structure of Manipur. As compared with other revolutionary leaders his educational qualification was not very high but his sense of degree of dedication and sacrifice for the party and ideology which he espoused was not inferior to that of other leaders. Through his limited educational experiences he tried at his best level to push forward the ideological concept of K.C.P. throughout the entire areas of Manipur. This was a unique leadership quality of Ibohanbi. In spite of all these developments, Ibohanbi Singh did not make any attempt to adopt the style of authoritarian type of the collective leadership. Therefore from all empirical and circumstantial evidences it can be suggested that the leadership pattern of the K.C.P. was always based on collective leadership system and practice of democratic principle within the party was clearly reflected in the nature of their working system.

## NOTES

1. Ganagrade, K.D.1974. *Emering Patterns of Leadership*. P.5.
2. Encyclopedia of Social Science. Volume 9-10. P.107.
3. Ibid. P.108.
4. Ibid. P.101.
5. Muzafer, Sharif. Ed. 1962. *Intergroups Relations and Leadership Approaches and Research in Industrial, Ethnic, Cultural and Political Areas*. New York.
6. Paul, Pigors. 1935. *Leadership or Domination*. Boston.
7. Stogill, Ralph M. Personal Factor Associated with Leadership. An article published in 1948.
8. *International Encyclopedia of Social Science*. Vol.9-10. P.107.

9. Ibid.
10. Ibid.
11. Bhusan. B. 1991. *Dictionary of Sociology*. P.160.
12. Stone, William F. 1974. *The Psychology of Politics*. P.144.
13. Bhusan. B. 1991. *Dictionary of Sociology*. P.160.
14. Ibid.
15. *Encyclopedia of Social Science*. Vol.13-14. P.504.
16. Ibid.
17. Sarangthem Mani Singh was the informant of the writer. Date of interview - 29.01.1988.
18. W.Tomba Singh was the informant of the writer. Date of interview- 13.9.1987 and 20.9.1987.
19. Ibid.
20. Pomeroy, W.J. *Guerrila and Counter Guerrilla Warfare*. P.52.
21. Constantine, R. Op.cit. P.118.
22. Ibid. P.90
23. Ibid. P.93.
24. A. Kamson of Kakhulong was the informant of the writer.
25. Ibid
26. N. Pahari was the informant of the writer.
27. Shri Sanasam Biramani Singh, ex-minister and childhood friend of late O.Sudhirkumar was the informant of the writer.
28. O. Gyaneshore Singh, a cousin of late Sudhir Singh, a retired teacher of Oriental college, Manipur was the informant of the writer.
29. S. Birmani Singh was the informant of the writer.
30. O. Gyaneshore was the informant of the writer.
31. Pillai, G.N. 1983. *Social Background of Political Leadership of India*. P.2.
32. Constantine, R. Op.cit. P.114.
33. Confessional statement of H. Mahashwor Singh, Chingamathak.
34. Singh. N. Pahari. 2002. *Eigi Diarydagi* (Manipuri). P.43.
35. *Dawn*. Vol. III. P.23.
36. *Sunday* (An English Weekly Journal).26 -07-1981. P.12.
37. Ibid.
38. Weber, Max. 1947. *The Theory of Social and Economic Organisation*. P.328.

39. Ibid.
40. *International Encyclpaedia of Social Science*. Vol. 1-2. P.387.
41. Straus, Claudi Levi. 1955. *The Structural Study of Myth- A Journal of America*. P.35.
42. Harvey, G.K. 1968. *Politics in Transitional Society*. New York. P.166.
43. *Sunday*. Op.cit. P.9.
44. Ibid. P.11.
45. A Leaflet issued by PREPAK on the XIX 'Foundation Day'. 09-10-1995. P.1.
46. A leaflet address to "All People for the upsing of the high time revolution" issued by Publicity Department, PREPAK. P.1.
47. Ibid.
48. Priyoshakhi Devi, mother of R.K. Tullachandra Singh was the informant of the writer (Date of interview – 150-4-2003).
49. Labango, P. 1968. *Politics in transitional Society*. New York. P.166.
50. Ibid.
51. Kangleipak Communist Party (K.C.P.). A pamphlet issued by K.C.P. signed by Ngamkham Bure Meitei, In-charge Chairman and Laishram Yaima Meitei, General Secretary.

# CHAPTER V

# IMPACTS

The main objective of a revolutionary movement is to bring about a sweeping change in a society. The outbreak of such type of movements may be treated as a landmark in the historical development of a given society. The significant aspect of the whole process of the movement was its implication in the future course of history of the particular country. It is a known fact that for every action there will be a reaction and for every historical event there will be a response and reaction. The reaction and the response are the best judge to any type of revolutionary movements and its natural judgment is the best measuring method of the performance of the revolutionary actors. It is true that the concept of 'sweeping change' would be possible only when the different elements in the society are actively involved either directly or indirectly to the cause of the movement. Here lies the important role of the revolutionary actors and their level of commitment and degree of integrity in the whole process of the movement. The idea of total change is possible only when the revolutionary actors play their positive role on the line of the desire of the society where the masses are actively involved.

The presence of the multiple dysfunctions in the society was the main factor for the creation of any type of disorder in the whole structure of the given social life. It is said that the outbreak of revolution was a direct response to the distinctive condition of the multiple dysfunction in the system of the society. On the other hand the 'dysfunction' in the social order is also a creation of the elements of the body of the society and it demands the response of either social change or revolution. In this respect we have to understand the role of the different elements in the society. Though it is not required to go into detail the elements in the society can be broadly divided into two i.e. the ruling elite and radical elements. From their natural character it can be observed that the main objective of the ruling elite group was to block all sorts of possible positive changes in the social process which might have given negative effect in their personal interest. The radical elements which the Marxist used to call 'revolutionary democrats' is constituted by the different groups of people in the society like peasant masses, semi proletarian urban population and nationalist intelligentsia. Their only desire was to bring the society in a more progressive and positive direction. So the unending dialogue between the two groups of elements in the society led to the outbreak of violent type of revolutionary movements. From these observations it can be said that the violent type of revolutionary movements occurred only when the possibilities of non-violent revolutionary changes was not occurring in the given society. In one way the outbreak of such type of movements may be taken as an appropriate response to the intransigent resistance of the ruling elite.

Giving a proper and befitting response to the resistance nature of the ruling elite cannot be possible without the involvement and participation of the common people. Since the radical elements are constituted by the multifaceted natural characters, it is not an easy task to bring them under a single roof of an umbrella. Numerically they are very strong and a large chunk of the members of the society is constituted by the people of this category but they have to be convinced or guided properly by the committed revolutionary actors who were acting as a torchbearer for a radical change. Here the question of relationship between revolutionary actors and common masses are highly involved. In his revolutionary theory Mao Tse-tung had compared the relationship between these two elements with the form of relationship between water and fish. It means that fish survive only in water and they have to swim according to the current of the watercourse. Likewise the degree of impetus, its importance and development in the progress of the revolutionary activities are entirely dependent on the positive support and involvement of the masses. In this respect the wisdom and revolutionary maturity of the participants can be discussed as the most important pre-requisite condition. Even when the natural process has created a revolutionary situation in a given society, if the revolutionary actors are not able to lead the masses in the proper and positive direction, the basic objective of the concept of sweeping change would become meaningless. Therefore the response of the masses is the most important for the success or failure of the movement and at the same time it is also an important yardstick for measuring the degree of wisdom and commitment of the revolutionary actors.

As has been stated above about the importance of the positive response of the masses on the way to the success of armed revolutionary movement, the basic issue is, under what type of approach the revolutionary actors would be able to receive the positive response of the masses. Here the character of the phenomena of the masses which may lead to the outbreak of any type of social movement have to be known very clearly. Many theories were advanced by different writers on the concept of mass phenomena and collective behaviour. They have categorized the mass phenomena into five major-sub types i.e., 1. Apathy, 2. Panic, 3. Mob, 4. Craze, and 5. Social movements[2]. Except the last category the first four is not directly related with the present work. Therefore the nature of the phenomena may be concentrated only in the last category. It is a fact that social movement has got different types of character. Among them the revolutionary movement is also another important branch. The basic concept of social movement is a "wide variety of collective attempt to bring about a change to certain social institution or to create an entirely new order".[3] So when the question of "collective attempt" is to be discussed the issue of the idea of positive response of the masses always come into the picture. To change or to create a new order means to abandon certain customs or practices and to adopt a different one. Therefore it is quite obvious that change would be possible only when the participants, who may be direct or indirect, have a tendency to change their ways and energies. It is also true that the nature of the masses, their attitude and character cannot be changed without any condition. Certain things and visions have to be placed before them so that they would have the opportunity to examine the situation in their best style and ways. The condition means the information to be given to the common people. In this connection Anthony F.C. Wallace pointed out four different types of information for the common people. According to him, 1. The information should describe a difference between individual's present situations and that which either has obtained in the past or very probably will obtain in the future. 2. The difference must be sufficient to constitute a dramatic gain or loss of important values. 3. The present or future loss must be perceived as an avoidable. or future gain as achievable if something is done and. 4. The information should be presented to the target group. approximately simultaneously.[4] He was of the view that the resultant action of these information would make the behaviour of the masses.

In the context of Manipur, Hijam Irabot Singh was the first historical personality who made an attempt to mobilize the masses in order to materialize his idea of a revolutionary change in the whole aspects of the society of Manipur. He asked the common people to involve and participate in the armed revolutionary movement which aimed for the establishment of a separate political identity based on the principle of a classless society. In order to carry out this revolutionary idea successfully he, with great care and calculation, tried to convince the people by using different political and social platforms. At least in Manipur his approach was a unique feature and such type of action may be treated as an important step for the emergence of collective behaviour among the masses. Like any other society, Manipur has got the character of plural society. So it was not an easy task for him to carry the whole masses in favour of his revolutionary idea. However, by dint of his tireless efforts he was able to establish hands with section of the peasant masses in the path of his revolutionary idea and later on he became an important spokesman of this class. His idea and concept for the welfare of the peasant society had produced a positive impact and it created an impression among the mind of the poorer section of the society that Irabot would be able to guide them towards a positive social life. On the basic foundation of this believe the peasant group of the state had extended a blanket support to him and also actively participated in his movement.

Yet, in spite of his best efforts he was not able to get support from the urban intellectual people of his time. "Still it is quite obscure to know the reasons behind it. One of the possible reasons might be the difference in the ideological concepts. The political and social outlook of Irabot was quite well known and his ideological concept perhaps was not acceptable to the leaders of the urban intellectual group. Rather he was branded as 'communist' by these elements. At that time there was a negative impression in the minds of the common people about the nature of the 'Communist Party'. The elements of the Congress Party in Manipur, which the Marxist termed as 'bourgeois democrats' always tried to create an impression to the common people that the elements of the Communist Party were all anti-social and criminal, etc. Though it is very difficult to give empirical evidences, but it is a fact that during the pre-merger period the common people always regarded the elements of Communist Party as 'Communist Michaba' (Communist man-eater), etc. These people always called 'Irabot Singh' as 'Communist Irabot'. At that time the implication of this nomenclature was quite negative. So if we analyze from the ground reality it can be observed that during the course of his movement Irabot had enjoyed little positive response from the masses of the urban area. The result of the 1948 election may be regarded as a very good measuring rod about the degree of the support of people of urban areas. Therefore lack of support from the urban intellectuals and common people who were regarded as the nerve centre of the whole society had produced serious negative development in the whole process of his revolutionary movement. On the whole Irabot was not able to get the positive response of the whole masses of the society of Manipur on the line of his expectation. However, the revolutionary movement led by H. Irabot Singh has produced a far-reaching positive impact in the future history and society of Manipur. The emergence of the idea of self-determination among the people was one of the best significant aspects of the movement. A strong desire for the preservation of the national identity of Manipur and its people was the immediate outcome of his revolutionary movement.

On the basic foundation of this concept a series of revolutionary movements appeared in the scene of political and social life of the common people at the initiative of different revolutionary organizations. The nature and character of the movements was almost on the same line of the political thesis i.e. preservation of the national identity of the people of Manipur. Though it is not required to go into detail it can be mentioned that the outbreak of the 'Meitei State Committee' as a revolutionary organisation was a significant development in the whole historical process of the post merger period of Manipur. The leaders of the movement, after having a good experience of the 1948 revolutionary activities, had launched the armed revolutionary movement with a new spirit and vision. In their approach they also adopted the same pattern which was adopted by their late leader. They also believed that no successful revolution could be launched without the help and co-operation from the people of hill areas. Therefore they made an attempt to reach a positive understanding with the leaders of the Naga Underground Movement. As a positive response to their attempt some tribal youths also participated in the movement. But in spite of their best attempt the revolutionary activities of the Meitei State Committee was not able to expand in large scale. Rather they were confined in a small pocket of area in the northern side of Imphal valley. On the other hand the propaganda machinery of the state government was so effective that they successfully branded the members of the Meitei State Committee as a band of anti-social elements who posses criminal mentality. So, the people of the urban area always looked to this revolutionary organization with different eyes. Thus the positive aspects of the organisation and their revolutionary concept was not able to reach the people in general and intellectual section of the society in particular.

When this was the condition of the Meitei State Committee another revolutionary organisation was established at the initiative of some section of the intellectual group of the urban area under the banner of the United National Liberation Front (UNLF). The organizer of this revolutionary front was intelligent and careful enough in handling the environmental situation of the society and government. Because of this result, though the organisation was started long time back, the awareness of the existence of this revolutionary party came to the knowledge of the general public in the later stage. No doubt the information of the establishment of the revolutionary front was confirmed only in a limited and negligible section of the common people. If the ground reality is to be studied it can be observed that the general people came to know about the existence of UNLF only after the massive arrest of the R.G.M. (Revolutionary Government of Manipur) volunteers. However, at that time the general public of the state, though they were not aware of the existence of another organisation in Manipur, were able to know a lot of information about the malpractice, mismanagement and degree of corruption in the administration, through a series of publication of PANMYL (Pan

Manipuri Youth League) At the initial stage the people were not able to know the real identity of this organisation. But gradually their real identity came to the knowledge of the common people. The 'Lamyanba' the monthly journal of the organisation, was the main contributor of the whole activities of PANMYL, and through this journal the common people came to know many untold stories particularly about the policy of the people of the Central Government and their negative attitude towards the people of Manipur. Thus from these critical analysis on the political, social and economic situation of the state the idea to foster and promote a distinctive national identity of the Manipuri people was increased tremendously among the people particularly among the younger generation of the society. However, the real identity of the PANMYL came to the surface only after the R.G.M. debacle. Whatever the case may be, the success of PANMYL as a great social force against the negative attitude of the ruling elite was undoubtedly a great contribution of the United National Liberation Front. The growth of the idea of national consciousness and to create a political atmosphere for the preservation of the separate identity of the Manipuri nationality may be treated as big contribution of the positive response of the common people. From this angle it can be suggested that though the people were not directly involved or participated in the process of movement their acceptance to the ideas for the preservation of the national identity itself may be treated as another form of positive response of the people. However, if we make an attempt to go a bit deeper into the level of maturity of political consciousness on the issue of the separatist tendencies among the minds of the common people it can be observed that the common people, though they were able to realize so many irregularities in the social, political and economic development of the state yet because of the lack of initiative and efforts of the activists, they were not able to give more attention to the issue of the separatist concept. Here we can find a basic difference between the common people and revolutionary activists in their process of interpretation on the concept of the preservation of the national identity of Manipuri people. At that time there was a strong movement for the establishment of responsible government in Manipur. All the people of Manipur, both old and young, women and children, were concentrating their mind and energy on this issue. Perhaps, the interpretation of the common people might be to establish an identity within the framework of Indian Constitution. But this does not mean that the response of the people was not there. Definitely the positive response of the common people was very much in the process of the preservation of the distinctive identity of Manipuri people.

The establishment of Revolutionary Government of Manipur (R.G.M.) and their revolutionary armed activities brought new sharp changes in the thinking process of the common people. It brought a new information to the knowledge of the common people about the strengthening and consolidation of the concept of separatist tendencies among some section of the common people particularly among the youths. It has already been mentioned in the previous chapters about the basic differences among the leadership of UNLF. Indeed there were no evidences in the ideological differences between UNLF and R.G.M. Both of them gave a strong emphasis on the strengthening of the Manipuri nationalism among the common people. The differences were only in their approach. Since the R.G.M. was established by the action-oriented elements who were forced to split from UNLF by their strong conviction, it strongly advocated that people's positive response would come only when they opened the trigger of armed revolution. But the mental makeup of the common people was not very clear. It seems that there was a lot of confusion in the minds of the people particularly on the political objective of the establishment of independent Manipur outside the Indian Union. As has been mentioned above, when the R.G.M. volunteers prepared for armed movement for an independent state of Manipur the minds of the majority of the people were confined to the issue of the establishment of a responsible government within the Indian union. Therefore large-scale involvement of the general people, either directly or indirectly to the cause of their revolutionary concept was not clearly visible by the naked eyes.

However the fruit of the revolutionary tree which was planted by M.S.C., UNLF and R.G.M. was successfully reaped by the People's Liberation Army Unit (Eastern Region), People's Revolutionary Party of Kangleipak (PREPAK) and Kangleipak Communist Party (KCP). After having a good experience of ups and downs in the process of the armed revolutionary movements the leaders of the new organizations had carefully put their revolutionary agendas on the tune of the desire of the people. The demand for the establishment of a classless society was a new aspect for the complete reformation of the ways of social life. The strong emphasis to promote and foster the downtrodden people like peasants and workers also gave a strong impetus to the revolutionary objectives of these revolutionary organizations. On the other hand the common people, particularly the younger group, after having a good experience on the political and administrative developments in the state right from the beginning of the post merger period and also after the establishment of a responsible government in the year 1972, began to feel some kind of negative outlook to the attitude of the central leaders of the Government of India. Therefore, sense of separatist tendency was developed in the minds of the younger generation people gradually. The spontaneous outburst of the idea of separatist tendency among the common people was clearly seen in the Kameng episode[5] in the year 1978. Such type of people's negative response never happened in the past. In the subsequent revolutionary movements also people's mind was always with revolutionary actors. The common masses began to regard all the revolutionary actors as patriots and the victim volunteers were regarded as 'martyrs'. The moral support of the people was so strong that even in the beginning of 1980s the machineries of the state government was not able to keep the law and order situation of the state in proper places. Even the activities of the life of the people in the main market places began to close before the sun set. This was the clear indication of the failure of the government on the one hand and good moral support of the common people to the cause of the revolutionary on the other.

From their official papers and leaflets it was quite clear that all the three revolutionary organizations had strongly emphasized for the improvement of peasant and workers group of the state. They also believed that they (peasants and workers) would be the spinal code of the whole anatomy of the revolutionary body. Perhaps they might have an impression that since the issue of the importance of peasants and workers had already placed for continuous discussion from the period of Hijam Irabot Singh, the revolutionary spirit of these group of people might be quite matured enough to make a spontaneous uprising for a change to a better society. N. Bisheshwor Singh had expressed his strong desire to make the revolutionary works of Peoples Liberation

Army (Eastern Region) as the 'Second Nanchang Uprising'. The 'Nanchang Uprising', indeed, was a great historical event that it made a turning point in the whole revolutionary movement in China. The peasants and workers were the main participants in the uprising. It is recorded that more than 15,000 (Fifteen thousand) peasants and workers were involved in this historic revolutionary event. They staged a coup at Nanchang on the 1st August, 1927 under the name of the Nationalist Left Wing and seized and controlled the city for three days[6]. Perhaps he might have an impression that the peasants, workers and other common people would definitely extend all sorts of support to the call of his revolutionary organisation. On the basis of this belief the P.L.A. Unit (Eastern Region) started revolutionary action by adopting the guerrilla type of revolutionary model. The same pattern and objective was also in the case of the Peoples Revolutionary Party of Kangleipak (PREPAK) and Kangleipak Communist Party (K.C.P.). From these evidences it can be observed that the basic objective of all these revolutionary organizations was to strengthen and consolidate the idea of a separate identity of Manipuri nation which the PREPAK and K.C.P. used to call 'Kangleipak national' and establishment of a classless society with an improvement of the condition of peasants and workers.

In this respect we can analyze the condition of the peasants of Manipur and their relationship with the landowners of both urban and rural areas. Compared with the other countries the degree of the suffering in the hands of landowners is extremely low. Even it can be observed that practically the peasants do not get any type of humiliation in the hands of landowners so far their economic life is concerned. It is a known fact that according to the traditional practices which have been continuing even today the peasants are still enjoying the maximum quantity of the paddy produced from the fields of the landowners. Though there is no unified pattern of the quantity of paddy to be given to the landowners for using their land the peasants are getting 80% to 90% of the total products. The relationship between landowner and peasant is maintained though a system called 'Lousal' (Lou – Paddy field, Sal or Sanba - to lend) i.e., the price of the lending paddy field under this traditional practices the landowner usually received minimum five and maximum twelve pots[7] of paddy per pari.[8] Sometimes the number of paddy pots is fixed on the basis of the agreement between tenants and landowners. That also depends on the degree of the fertility of the particular paddy field. In the wet cultivation areas the minimum quantity of production of paddy was between sixty to eighty pots per pari. In the fertile area the quantity of production sometimes reached hundred pots. Whatever the case of the degree of the quantity of production may be, the landowners received only the minimum quantity of number of paddy pots which were fixed as convention from the very early period. In the real sense of the term, economically the peasants were not suffering in the hands of landowners. This was a significant contradiction from the conditions of other areas. Actually, from the study of the proportion of suffering peasants, they were not suffering from the real hard life of the peasants which was noticed in other parts of the world. The quantum of the suffering of the peasants in other areas was quite evidenced by the degree of their participation and involvement in the violent type of revolutionary movement which occurred in their respective areas. On the other hand the degree of participation and involvement of the peasants section of the society of Manipur in compared with other areas were extremely low. Even during the revolutionary period of Hijam Irabot the peasant's involvement was confined only in a limited area where most of the paddy fields belong to the members of the royal family group. From their nature it can be observed that perhaps they were not able to come out from the conflicting nature of feudal character which was practiced as a political or social system for quite long time. Rather majority of this group were quite aloof as if nothing was known to them.

On the other hand the role of the workers in the process of the historical development of Manipur was also not visible. Since there were neither big nor middle scale industries in Manipur, the problem of the workers particularly in their relationship with industrial owners group was not a social issue. So the question of suffering of the workers in the real sense of the term was not in the case of Manipur and since there were no workers group the issue of this group of people as a strong social class, as we have seen in other areas was not the case of Manipur. Therefore the role of workers as expected as a strong revolutionary force in Manipur was not in existence. In short, it can be said that because of the given situation the degree of the awareness of the existing social, political and economic conditions among the peasants and also the small section of workers was not to the expectation of the revolutionary actors.

As has been stated above about the basic objective of the top leader of P.L.A. Unit (Eastern Region), the only dream of Bisheshwor Singh was to make the P.L.A. Unit (Eastern Region) movement as a "Second Nanchang Uprising". He thought that the large-scale involvement and participation of peasants' section of the society would be in the process of their movement. However if we analyze the real position it can be observed that the mass participation as desired by Bisheshwor was not clearly visible. No doubt sense of involvement and idea for the improvement of their social and economic status was very much there yet the feeling of the participation physically were not in their mind. This was the contradiction in the nature of the peasant masses of Manipur and other parts of the world. In this respect many social scientists of the state are of the view that their lack of sense of awareness and involvement in the process of the revolutionary change in the society was mainly because of their economic position. They were of the opinion that economically the peasants of Manipur did not reach the degree of financial hardship as was seen in other parts of the world. They were not at the level of slavery. They were able to manage to have self-sufficient economy in their respective families. They did not receive any type of negative attitude from their landowners. There was no social barrier between the peasants and landowners. In fact under the prevailing economic and social circumstances the agenda of the concept of the emancipation of their social position may not be reflected in the minds of the peasants section of Manipur. Perhaps this aspect also may be treated as one of the reasons for having the lack of feeling in the sense of participation and involvement in the process of the revolutionary movement in the society of Manipur.

Apart from the peasants and workers all the revolutionary organizations also paid due respect and importance to the role played by the middle class educated people in the historical process of the growth of national identity of Manipuri people. The educated middle class here signifies the persons who received higher education through the medium of English and engaged in different recognized professions grown as a result of western education and capitalist economy[9]. It is a fact that this group of people played an important role to the growth of political consciousness in the state and to reach certain conceptual framework about the national identity among the common people was also their significant contribution. But they are not united and always have a critical eye in every historical development. So there is imperative on the part of the revolutionary actors to have a clear observation and study about their attitude towards the new developments. If we go back to the history of the growth of political consciousness in Manipur it can be observed that this idea flourished only with the establishment of Nikhil Hindu Manipuri Mahasabha in the year 1934. The first political party in Manipur came into being in the year 1938. The persons and leaders who initiated for this new development were all influenced by the basic political ideas of Indian culture and tradition. On the one hand they expressed their desire to have a separate political identity on the basic principle of democracy. No doubt they were all against feudal system of administration. But on the other they were also not in favour of the complete removal of the philosophical link with Indian culture and tradition. The important role of this group of people and their influence continued for quite a long time. This was also one of the reasons for lack of support of H. Irabot Singh from urban areas when he put a political agenda for self-determination. In fact there is no second question about the importance of intellectual group of the society in the process of the success of the revolution. But it depends on the relationship between the revolutionary actors and intellectuals. The relationship is not at the level of personal but at the level of philosophy, concept and objective and the attitude of the revolutionary actors towards them is also another indispensable one. P.L.A Unit (Eastern Region) said, "we realize that without the participation of revolutionary intellectual no revolution can be successful. Therefore, they should not be neglected but are to be united"[10]. From history it is quite clear that there was no unity among the intellectual circles particularly on the issue of self-determination. This was clearly evidenced during the revolutionary period of Hijam Irabot Singh. The contradiction was on the issue of interpretation. Irabot wanted to establish national identity outside the Indian Union whereas the other intellectuals thought that identity could be established within Indian Constitution. This debate continued even in the post-merger period also.

The impact of the debate among the intellectuals had severely reflected in the revolutionary process of Meitei State Committee. Taking the advantage of the confused situation among the intellectuals the government successfully branded this revolutionary organisation group as anti-social elements. In the midst of this debate the United National Liberation front (UNLF) was established at the initiative of some young educated people. As has been stated above the organisation took special care of the political agenda of their organisation and their revolutionary activities. Therefore, they took a slow pace in mobilizing people. Because of these reasons the existence of this organisation came to the knowledge of the people in a late stage. This is a clear indication of the level of the maturity of the organisation in the study of the social environment of the state. When the revolutionary activities of the Revolutionary Government of Manipur (R.G.M.) came into being on the surface the intellectual group of the society did express their view neither in favour of the party nor against it. Rather they were in deep confusion. In the meantime, a new intellectual group emerged and they also began to challenge the ideas of those groups of people who belong to the post-merger school of political thought. But if we go into the reality aspect it can be observed that though they were not in favour of the old political thought but practically they could not come out openly with a clear concept of identity. No doubt, they expressed their unhappiness, they also lamented for the negative attitude of the Central Government, but still they cannot give a clear political and social line to the common people. Because of this reason common people were not able to see a clear-cut concept about the society of Manipur. Perhaps this development might be because of economic hardship faced by this group of people. Though it is not possible to give any empirical data the circumstantial evidences show that the impact of unclear stand of intellectual groups in the society had also been indirectly reflected in the course of movement of organizations. Bisheshwor Singh, during his revolutionary period, said that intellectual couldn't lead the revolution, until they are re-educated by the objective realities and adopt the hardship of the revolution by transforming their nature of subjectivism[11]. In this respect it can be observed that the importance of intellectuals in the process of revolutionary change is not on the question of leadership but on the issue of the utilization of their wisdom and academic guidance. Bisheshwor said the real force of the revolution i.e. reliable and motive force was the working class[12]. But the basic question is that in the real sense of the term there was no working class in Manipur as we have seen in other parts of the world. Manipur was peasants' masses. And who would lead them to revolution? No doubt they would be led by the revolutionary actors. And who would give the proper guidance to them? Indeed it is to be guided by the intellectuals or educated middle class people. When the minds of the intellectual people was in the midst of confusion or when they refused to give their proper academic analysis on every aspect of the society, definitely it would create some hurdle in the process of the revolutionary movements. Therefore, like peasants and workers, the role of intellectuals is also equally important in the path of the successful revolutionary movement. Here the role of the revolutionary actors is very important.

Whatever the case may be the outbreak of revolutionary movement is a very important landmark in the changing social process of the state. No doubt it is a long and difficult process. During this period common people as well as revolutionary actors have to face many struggles both from inside and outside. By giving justification of the armed movement, Bisheshwor said "mobilisation of the people without armed struggle is an opportunist, and armed struggle led by a wrong leadership is harmful and dangerous to the revolutionary cause, as it leads the people in astray. Armed struggle under correct leadership is the best form and the most scientific method of mobilisation and it will open a new chapter in the history of our revolution."[13] Here lies a very big question on who would take the most correct leadership. What would be the criteria of a correct leadership? The answers of these basic issues may be expected from the revolutionary actors of the past.

Though, the large scale involvement and physical participation of the masses in the process of the revolutionary movement as anticipated by the revolutionary leaders was not clearly witnessed by the common people, their work has produced a far reaching impact on the future history Manipur. The unhappiness and dissatisfaction among the people of Manipur particularly towards the new political and economic development after the year 1949, have already been discussed in previous chapters. So, the political and economic condition which was developed in Manipur after its integration with India was the responsible factor for the growth of separatist tendency among the younger generation people. This issue came to the knowledge of the policy makers of the Government of India by the genuine action of the revolutionary organizations. It is a fact that the integration of Manipur with India and its resultant impact was not a happy development both for pro-merger and anti-merger groups. For the people of anti-merger group this new development was so unexpected whereas for the people of pro-merger group the subsequent development was so disappointing and the new trend was against their expectation. Their only desire was to establish a responsible government on the same pattern as other Indian states, when the Government of India put Manipur as a 'Part C' State of the Indian Constitution. This group of people was quite restless and started a political movement for the establishment of a responsible government. But the attitude of the Government of India towards the political demand of Manipur was not to the tune of the desire of the people of this state. The deliberate ignorance of the Central Government to the genuine political demand of Manipur forced the radical youths of this state to launch armed revolutionary movement for the preservation of a separate political identity of Manipur outside the Indian Union. The first reaction was started by the Meitei State Committee (MSC) in the last quarter of 1960s. Then the establishment of the United National Liberation Front (UNLF) with a clear political ideology of Manipuri nationalism had further cemented the idea of self-determination. Under the banner of this ideology, silent campaign had been successfully launched among the desperate people of Manipur. Their campaign had further rekindled the fire of revolution among the younger generation of Manipur. Then the armed action of the Revolutionary Government of Manipur (RGM) had sharpened the edge of the separatist tendency which was already in the minds of the young people of Manipur.

Indeed, their militant action had forced the members and leaders of the policy making body of the Central Government to open their eyes. After having the experience of the armed revolutionary movement they began to realize the degree of unhappiness of the people and their political determination which was deliberately ignored for a long time. Then they began to give special attention to the cause of Manipur and they also came to know the importance of this place from the strategic point of view. In the meantime a lot of political pressure also began to come in favour of the cause of the political movement of Manipur. This new trend in the political attitude of the Central Government was undoubtedly a great contribution of the armed revolutionary movement, that their action had forced the central leaders to change their attitude. Thus after having seen the dangerous trend of the separatist tendencies and possible impact in the entire study of the North-Eastern Region, Government of India granted to establish a full-fledged state in Manipur, the same political status of other states in India, in the year 1972. In fact the establishment of a responsible government in Manipur within the framework of Indian Constitution was not the political agenda of the revolutionary organisation but this new political development which was denied for quite long time by the central leaders of India, was undoubtedly a significant impact of their action.

Apart from this new political development the revolutionary actions of the organizations also had produced a lot of positive impact on other developmental aspects of the state. The establishment of a University and a Medical College in Manipur was also undoubtedly a big contributory impact of their action. No doubt the demand for the establishment of a University was very much there but because of their negative attitude the central leaders did not make any response to it in spite of having the pre-requisite infrastructure. It was only when the revolutionary organizations began to open their revolutionary weapons that the central leaders realized the importance of an institution of higher learning in the state. This was also in the case of the medical college. From these educational institutions the people of Manipur are getting maximum opportunity for the betterment of the future society. If there was no exchange of fire the establishment of these two educational institutions might be a futile attempt either of the political parties of the state or social organizations.

To bring every issue of Manipur to the limelight of the national mainstream of India was also another important significant impact of the revolutionary movements in this state. There was an impression among the younger generation that the people of the mainland India as well as the leaders of the Central Government had deliberately ignored and neglected the importance of the Manipuri people as a part of the Indian Union. It was a very important sentimental issue for every Manipuri. This was also one of the basic causes for the growth of separatist tendency among the young educated people. After having this experience of negligence the young educated people thought that to establish a separate identity outside the Indian Union was the only way to protect, preserve and foster the rich traditional culture and pride of Manipur state. On the basis of this understanding and with an objective to establish a separate political identity of Manipuri people outside the Indian constitution, the revolutionary organizations had launched their separatist movements.

The policy makers of the Government of India was also fully aware of the minds of the people of Manipur. Perhaps they also have appreciated the feeling of the Manipuri people particularly younger generation group. Then they began to change their attitude and started to give recognition to the value and importance of the Manipuri people in the form of the material development. The establishment of a dance academy under the sponsorship of Central Government was a good indicator of the attempt of the Government to promote and foster the traditional culture of this place. Apart from this they also began to give other recognition to the individuals who delivered the best in the field of art and culture and their importance was widely respected at the national level. Apart from this the Government of India also began to recognize the skill of the youths of Manipur in the field of sports. In order to promote the sports culture they extended all sorts of possible infrastructure in this state. With the help of these infrastructures the youths of Manipur were able to compete successfully in the field of sports with the youths of other states at the national level competitions. In addition to this many social scientists of the national level began to take keen interest in the history, society and environmental conditions of the place. Now they have taken intensive research work in order to discover the importance of the people of Manipur at the national level.

Thus the emergence of these revolutionary movements had produced a significant impact not only on her future history but also on her historical identity. Now the issue of her separate identity is widely known at the international level and the problem of the violation of human rights, which happened in the past and what is happening now come to the knowledge of the international agencies.

If the totality of the process of the movement is to be analyzed it can be seen that although they received so many drawbacks and loopholes in the course of the movement and lapses in the process of understanding with the common people, their ideological principles, agendas and objectives had laid a remarkable basic foundation for the growth of historical identity of the state of Manipur in particular and North East Region in general. Whatever the case may be the outbreak of these revolutionary movements had given a significant contribution to the ongoing historical process for the fostering and preservation of the national identity of Manipuri people.

## NOTES

1. Kely, G.A. and C.W. Brown Jr. Ed. 1973. *Struggle in the State, Source and Pattern of World Revolutionary.* P.93.
2. *International Encyclopedia of Social Science.* Vol. 10. P.54.
3. Ibid. Vol.13-14. P.445.
4. Ibid. Vol. 9.57
5. 'Kameng Episode.' It is a very important event of the revolutionary history of the last part of nineteenth seventies. In this episode the joint operational force had killed some revolutionary members of both PREPAK and P.L.A. The event occurred on 12th November, 1978.
6. Emmanuel Hsu. *The Rise of Modern China.* 6th Ed.
7. It is traditional weight measuring system mainly used in the trade of paddy. One pot of paddy, in local language 'Fou Pot', is constituted by two 'Sangbai'. It is name of a basket. Sixty-four 'Utongs' constitute one 'Sangbai'.
8. Pari i.e., 1pari =2$^1/_2$ acres of of land.
9. Misra, B.B. 1961. *The Indian Middle Classes: Their Growth in Modern Time.* P.147.
10. *Dawn.* Vol.II. P.11.
11. Ibid.
12. Ibid. P.12.
13. Ibid.

## *APPENDIX I*

# P.L.A. MISGUIDES YOU

1. To restore normal life in the State, especially in the valley area, the army is now engaged in picking out the anti-social element and extremists such as the member of the so-called PLA and such other characters who are the source of the disturbance.
2. The fact that whatever the army is now doing for the protection of the life and property of loyal citizens and in the best interest of the innocent-loyal public needs no emphasis.
3. Had not the so called PLA and other dacoit gangs started making the lives of the people in Manipur insecure by their indiscriminate looting and killing, it should not have been necessary for the army to come in. Therefore, any inconvenience caused by the army operation, if any, the PLA is to be blamed. In other words, all the present misery had been brought about by the PLA and other extremists.
4. Instead of holding themselves responsible, the PLA is now trying to deceive the people by branding this operation of the army against them [P.L.A.], as "an act of invasion by the Indian Army which is false.
5. The people of Manipur know very well that in 1949 the princely state of Manipur like many other princely states opted for merger into the Union of India. And this state is a part and parcel of Indian Union according to the wishes of the people, which is irrevocable.
6. India is a Sovereign, Secular, Socialist, Democratic country and we cannot allow some misguided youths to subvert it in this manner.
7. This kind of movement have come and gone even in some parts of the north-eastern region alone and left the development programmes of those regions retarded, many killed and many others left suffering for nothing, thereby simply multiplying the sufferings of the people by manifold.

8. This problem of disturbed law and order situation under which many innocent people suffer and live a panic striken life could be brought to an early end before more lives and areas are affected by the continued full co-operation of the people to the government. To do this the people should refuse any sort of assistance asked for by the lawless elements even under threat and put up a strong resistance by bringing such matters to the Government authorities for immediate action.

9. The army is only assisting the popularly elected State Government of Manipur for early restoration of normal life in the interest of the welfare of the general public. It is, therefore, appealed to the people to extend full co-operation against these lawless elements. The army will be here with us till they finish their job.

GOVERNMENT OF MANIPUR

---

*APPENDIX II*

## APPEAL

The topmost leader of the out-lawed Peoples' Liberation Army, Shri N. Bisheshwor Singh was apprehended by the Security Forces in the evening of 6/7/81 at Teckcham village near Wangjing from their secret hide out. Along with him another active member of P.L.A., Shri Sarat alias Sashi was also captured.

In the encounter with the Security Forces in that village in the evening of 6/7/81 other seven hard-core P.L.A. members S/Shri Kabichandra, Rajen Macha, Indrajit, Khogen, Shanti, Biramangol and Inao were killed after heavy exchange of fire. Some arms and ammunitions including sophisticated ones and printing blocks were also recovered from them.

With the above happenings, we hope that our misguided brothers realize that the path of violence cannot lead to good for anyone. On behalf of the Government we earnestly appeal to everyone to cooperate with us to maintain peace that all our energies can be directed towards the development and well-being of our people of Manipur.

Rishang Keishing
Chief Minister
Manipur.

**Imphal,**
**July 8, 1981.**

*APPENDIX III*

## CASH REWARD FOR CAPTURE/ INFORMATION LEADING TO CAPTURE THE MEITEI EXTREMISTS

The Government of Manipur has announced cash reward for capture/ information leading to capture the Meitei Extremists as per details given below:-

| Name of Extremists | Capture alive | Capture dead | Information leading to capture alive/ dead |
|---|---|---|---|
| 1. Elangbam Surjaboro Singh, S/o. Leiren Singh of Pishum Ningom Leirak. | Rs. 25,000/- | Rs. 20,000/- | Rs. 20,000 |
| 2. Soibam Temba Singh, S/o. Nodiachand Singh of Thongju Village. | - do - | - do - | - do - |
| 3. Thoudam Kunjabihari Singh, S/o. Gandha Singh of Nameirakpam Leikai. | - do - | - do - | do |
| 4. Chirom Ranjit Singh, S/o. Patho Singh of Singjamei Chirom Leikai. | - do - | - do - | - do - |
| 5. Naorem Rajen (O) Rajen Achouba Singh, S/o. Komol Singh of Naorem Leikai. | - do - | - do - | - do - |
| 6. R.K. Tullachandra Singh, S/o Rochon Singh of Thangmeiband Kabrabam Leikai. | - do - | - do - | - do - |

*APPENDIX IV*

# P.L.A. PRESS NOTE
# (Translation into English)

For the first time we have opened our 'militia team'. We opened this team with an advice of Ojha N. Bisheshwor Singh the only leader of both party and army of our organisation. The duty of the 'militia team' is to assist the main force (P.L.A.) and to give defeat the 'Mayang Army' in guerrilla warfare. As a first step this team was able to rescue Thongam Kabichandra the representative of party (party representative) from the hand of the enemy. As a mark of happiness to this victory P.L.A.'s official journal 'Nongallakpa' (Dawn) have been presented to the people. Within a short time this journal will publish in Manipuri language (Meiteilon) and other languages.

# BIBLIOGRAPHY

## A. PRIMARY SOURCES

A leaflet addressed to all people for the uprising of the high time revolution.' A leaflet issued by Publicity Department, Government of Kangleipak, PREPAK.

Administrative Report of Manipur, 1945-55.

Administrative Report of Manipur, 1957.

Administrative Report of Manipur, 1960-61.

An announcement of cash reward for capture/information leading to the capture of Meitei extremist, issued by the Government of Manipur.

Annual Administration Report of Manipur, 1946-57.

Annual Administrative Report of Manipur, 1967-68.

Annual Administrative Report of Manipur, 1972-73.

Appeal (An official leaflet issued by the Government of Manipur in the name of Shri Rishang Keishing, the Chief Minister of Manipur on July 8, 1981).

Committee and Commission in India 1947-73. Vol. I.

Confessional Statements.

Criminal Miscellaneous Petition No. 221 of 1971 Union Territory vs. Yumnam Biren Singh and others.

*Dawn.* (A publication of P.L.A.). Vol. I/II/III.

File No. 8/6 (3) /79 D.I.G., C.I.D. Secret Police Department, Government of Manipur.

Indianised Politics in the South East Asia. A pamphlet.

Kangleipak Communist Party (K.C.P.). A pamphlet signed by Ng. Babu Meitei in charge of Chairmen and Laishram Yaima Meitei, General Secretary.

Kangleipak Communist Party (KCP). A pamphlet issued by the National Political Advisory Red Army, signed by N. Babu Meitei, in-charge Chairman.

Lalhouba Naharolsingda Appeal. (An appeal to the revolutionary youths). Issued by Government of Manipur, 13.6.1980.

Letter from Shri Prakash to Maharaja of Manipur. 4.7.1949.

Letter from Shri Prakash, Governor of Assam to Maharaja of Manipur. 19.9.1949.

Letter from the 23 R.G.M. Volunteers in jail to the Lt. Governor of Manipur.

Manifesto of People's Revolutionary Party of Kangleipak, (PREPAK.).

Mannaba Khunnaigi Lamda PREPAK. (PREPAK in the midst of war for a classless society). A pamphlet issued by PREPAK.

Memorandum submitted by the Manipur Youths Assembly Demand Committee to the President of India for the restoration of Responsible Government in Manipur.

Memorandum submitted to the President of India on 3rd April, 1960 by Assembly Demand Coordinating Committee, Manipur.

Memorandum submitted to the State Reorganisation Commission, April 1954.

Miyamda revolutionarygi paojel. (A revolutionary message to the people). Pamphlet issued by PREPAK.

9th October 1995. XIX Foundation Day Celebration of People's Revolutionary Party of Kangleipak (PREPAK). A pamphlet issued by the Department of Publicity and Propaganda.

Oppose Indian Annexation Month. September 21 to October 15, 1994. Published by United National Liberation Front (UNLF).

P.L.A. Misguides You. (A pamphlet issued by the Government of Manipur.).

P.L.A. na miyamda laothokchaba. (An announcement to the people by P.L.A.)

P.L.A. na miyamda lauthokchaba, (An announcement of P.L.A. to the people). A pamphlet issued by P.L.A.

People's Revolutionary Party of Kangleipak. Issued by 'Red Army', PREPAK.

Police amasung arm forces singda PREPAK na khanghalli. (An address to the police and armed forces personnels by PREPAK) issued by the Publicity Dept., Government of Kangleipak PREPAK.

Political Thesis of Manipur. A pamphlet.

PREPAK Ningtam Landa 'Phingang Lanmi'. (Red Army in the liberation war of PREPAK.) Pamphlet issued by Propaganda Committee of PREPAK.

Secret documents of Jananeta Hijam Irabot. Vo. I. Published by Manipur State Archives, Director of Arts and Culture, Government of Manipur.

Secret Memorandum No. 1601 PI. 1 dated 25.6.1949 from Maharaja Bodhachandra to Sri Prakash, Governor of Assam.

Statement of Central Committee of the United National Liberation Front (UNLF) issued on the 24th November, 1992 on the occasion of 28th Anniversary.

The 9th October, The 16th Foundation Anniversary of People's Revolutionary Party of Kangleipak (PREPAK) and its' Armed Wing People's Red Army, 1992. (A pamphlet issued by the Information Publicity Department of PREPAK.).

The Basic Issue. (Federation is the need of the hour). Published by Federal Party of Manipur. 1993.

The Gazetteer of Manipur, 1950.

United National Liberation Front na miyamda sengdokchaba. (A clarification by U.N.L.F. to the people.) A pamphlet issued on 12.5.1992.

Why Manipuris Demand Right to Self-Determination. Published by UNLF 1996.

Why Responsible Government in Manipur. Published by Statehood Demand Coordinating Committee.

## B. NEWS PAPERS (MANIPURI AND ENGLISH)

*Amrit Bazar Pratika* (English).

*Freedom* (English).

*Huiyen Lanpao* (Manipuri).

*Indian Express* (English). 30th October, 1980.

*Khollao* (Manipuri).

*Manipur Mail* (English).

*Paojel* (Manipuri).

*Prajatantra* (Maniuri).

*Resistence* (English weekly).

*Statement* (English).

## C. JOURNALS (ENGLISH AND MANIPURI)

*Anouba* (Manipuri monthly journal). December, 1966. Anouba (Manipuri monthly journal). December, 1966.

*Lamyanba* (A monthly Manipuri journal). Published by Panmyl. Lamyanba (A monthly Manipuri journal). Published by Panmyl.

*Lanmei Thanbi* (Manipuri monthly journal). October, 1985. Vol. III. No. 6.Lanmei Thanbi (Manipuri monthly journal). October, 1985. Vol. III. No. 6.

*Sunday*. 26th July, 1981

*Sunday* (English Weekly magazine published by Ananda Bazar Publication, Calcutta, 9-15th May, 1982)

## D. ARTICLES

Arun, M.C. 1993. The Problem of Insurgency in India: A Philosophical Analysis.

Burman, B. K. Roy. North East India: An overview. *Mainstream*. December 6, 1980.

Dena, Lal. 1993. Sources and Political violence: An enquiry.

Dena, Lal. Manipur and British Paramountcy.

Dena, Lal. Roots of Separatist Movement in North East India.

Ghose, P. K. Organisational Structure of Revolutionary Secret Society: Anushilan Samity, 1901-1918. *Bengal: Past and Present*. July – December. 1978.

Gokulchandra, Kh. 1993. Freedom and Responsibility (Search for ethnic identity, independence and responsibility).

Horam, M. 1992. Safeguarding the territorial integrity of Manipur.

Insurgency in Manipur: Search for an answer. 9th September, 1989.

Joykumar, N. 1991. Manipurna Bharatta Tingkhibagi Mityeng Ama. (Manipuri).

Kabui, Gangmumei.1981. Insurgency in Manipur Valley.

Muivah, Ng. 1997. Safeguarding the territorical integrity of Manipur.

Ngahak, Van Lal. 1993. Freedom, Political violence and Terrorism.

Saratchandra, P. I.A.S. Insurgency in Manipur: Search for an answer.

Sharma, L. Bishwanath. 1993. Freedom and Responsibility: A Semantic Analysis.

Shymkanhai, Ksh. 1982. The Merger of Manipur with India.

Singh Lt. Col. H. Bhuban (Retd.). Insurgency in Manipur: Search for an answer.

Singh, S. Bharatbushan. Insurgency in Manipur: Search for an answer.

## E. BOOKS (ENGLISH)

Arendt, Hannah. 1963. *On Revolution.* New York.

Batalov, E. 1983. *Lenin's Theory on Revolution.* Moscow.

Bhusan, B. 1991. *Dictionary of Sociology.*

Briston, C. 1965. *The Anthology of Revolution.* New York.

Brutents, K.N. *National Liberation Revolutions Today.* Part II.

Burlatsky, Feddor. 1976. *Mao Tse-Tung, An Ideological and Psychological Portrait.*

Carnichael, Stokely and Charles Hamilton. 1968. *Black Power.* Jonathan Cape, London.

Chang, Ronald Yena-Lin. Ed. 1973. *The Sociology of Revolution: Reading on Political Upheavals on Popular Unrest.* Chicago.

Cohen, A. S. 1975. *Theories of Revolution: An Introduction.* University of Lanchester.

Constantine, R. *Manipur: Maid of the Mountain.*

*Dictionary of Psychology.* Progress Publishers. 1984.

*Dictionary of Scientific Communism.* Progress Publishers. 1984.

Ellwood, Charles A. 1920. *Sociology and Its Psychological Aspects.* New York.

*Encyclopedia of Social Sciences.* Vol. 13-14.

Ganagrade, K.D. 1974. *Emerging Pattern of Leadership.*

Gavlin, M. and L. Kazakova.1980. *Elitist Revolution or Revolution of the Masses.*

Goole, Willaim J. Ed. *The Dynamics for Modern Society.* New Delhi.

Gough, Kathleen and Hari P. Sharma. Ed. 1973. *Imperialism and Revolution in South Asia.*

Gross, Felik. 1958. *The Seizure of Political Power in a Century of Revolution.* New York.

Hegopian, Mark. N. 1978. *Regime, Movements, Ideologies: A Comparative Introduction to Political Science.* New York.

Hsu, Immanuel C.Y. *The Rise of Modern China.* 6th Ed.

*Jawaharlal Nehru's Speech.* Vo. I

Kelly, George A. and Clifford W. Brown Jr. Eds. 1970. *Struggle in the State Sources on Pattern of World Revolution.* U.S.A.

Lenin, V.I. 1972. *State and Revolution.* Moscow.

Lenin, V.I. 1983. *What is to be done.* Moscow. 1983.

Lenin, V.I. *Collected Works.* Vol. 26.

Lenin, V.I. *Collected Works.* Vol. 33.

Lipset, Seymour Martin. 1959. *Political Man: the Social Base & Politics.*

Majumdar, R.C., H.C. Roychoudhary, A.K. Dutta. 1965. *An Advance History of India.*

Martin, Everall D. 1920 *The Behaviour of Crowd. A Psychological Study.* New York.

Misra, B.B. 1961. *The Indian Middle Classes, Their Growth in Modern Times.*

Narahari, Lt. General N.S. (Retd.). 2002. *Security Threat to North East India; The socio Ethnic Tensions.*

National Research Centre (NCR). *Youth Mental Unrest in Manipur.*

Nayar, Lt. General V.K. (Retd.). 2000. *Low Intensity Conflict of India.* New Delhi.

Nkrumaha, Kwame.1973. *Neo-colonialism, The Last Stage of Imperialism.*

Pettee, George Sawyer. 1971. *The Process of Revolution.* New York.

Pillai, G. Narayna. 1983. *Social Background of Political Leadership in India.*

Pomeroy, William J. *Guerilla and Counter Guerilla Warfare.*

Ravga, N. G. 1949. *The Revolutionary Peasants.*

Ravga, N. G. 1985. *The Revolutionary Process in the East: Past and Present.*

Rejai, Mastafa Rejai. 1973. *The Strategy of Political Revolution*. New York.

Roy, Sibnarary. *For a Revolution from Below*. India: Minerva.

Ruddin, Badar. 1991. *Administrative Change in Manipur After 1891.*

Rude, George. 1959. *The Crowd in the French Revolution.*

Sergai (Prof.) and P. Novaselov. Ed. 1981. *Problems of Communist Movement*. Moscow.

Singh, Ibotombi. (Ed.). *Congress and Manipur Statehood.*

Singh, N. Joykumar. 2002. *Colonialism to Democracy: History of Manipur 1819-1972.*

Singh, Nameirakpam Bisheshwor. 1986. *The last Expression on My Death Bed.*

Singh, Phanjoubam Tarapot. 1993. *Insurgency Movement in North-East India.*

Stone, William F. 1974. *The Psychology of Politics.*

Strauss, Claude Levi. 1935. *The Structural Study of Myth.*

Webber, Max. 1947. *The Theory of Social and Economic Organisation.*

Wetheim, W. F. 1974. *Evolution or Revolution. The Rising wave of Emancipation*. London.

Wilkinson, Paul. 1971. *Social Movements.*

Wolfenstien, E. Victor. 1971. *The Revolutionary Personality, Lenin, Trotsky and Gandhi*. New Jersey, U.S.A.

**F. BOOKS (MANIPURI)**

Ancient text (Puya) – *Sanmahi Laikan.*

Chhatradhari, S. 1997. *Manipurgi Itihasta Irabot.*

Khomdon, J.K. 1995. *Khunnaigi Saktamdagi.*

*Macha Leima*. Vol. I. Issue I. 1997. Published by Manipur Chanura Leishem Marup.

Mangang, P. Labango. 1997. *Kangleipakta Revolution.*

*Meihum Morok*. Published by Kanglei Yaol Kanna Lup, 7th Edition. 2002.

Naga, G.L. Geising R. 1986. *Free Naga Revolution.*

Pahari, N. 2002. *Eigi Dairidagi.*

Pan Manipur Youth League. 1993. *Bharatki Loilam Manipur:* 25th Anniversary Publication.

Sarin, H.K. *Bharatki Awang Nongpok Lamdamda Lalhoubagi Irang* (Translated from English to Manipuri).

Sharma, Atombapu. *Bijoy Panchalli.*

Singh, A. Samarendro. 1968. *Judge Sahebki Imung.*

Singh, Mangol. 1973. *Guerilla Warfare* (Manipuri).

Yengkhoiba, Sanajaoba. 1996. *Manipurda Indian Governmentki Karamba Mityeng.*

# INDEX